# Warrior

# Philosophy

in

# GAME OF THRONES

## Also by Francis Briers:

A little book on finding your Way:
Zen and the Art of Doing stuff

## And soon to be released...

My Tao Te Ching: A Fools Guide to Effing the Ineffable

The Art of Dad-Fu

Somatic Presence

Karate Principles for Life

# Warrior

# Philosophy

## in

## GAME OF THRONES

Francis Briers

Warriors of Love Publishing

ISBN 978-0-9567799-1-5

A copy of this book has been deposited with the British Library.

Published by Warriors of Love (WOL) Publishing

**Cover designed and illustrated by Rob Dreaming:
www.knightsofgaia.com**

# Acknowledgements

Firstly I must acknowledge George R. R. Martin for writing a truly epic series of books without which this book would have had to take a very different form! Next of course is the awesome team at HBO who have created a truly brilliant TV production of this story. It really is such beautiful work.

More personally I have been assisted, supported, taught, mentored, and loved by many people over the years in the Warrior's path, my personal development, writing, and living. My mother, Lyn, and my father, Fred have always been so unconditionally supportive, and my wife Miche and son Samson who are continuing that tradition! I also want to make a special mention of Rob Dreaming who created the beautiful cover art. You have helped to keep me inspired to finish what I started here with your awesomeness! Thanks brother.

My various martial companions over the years, and particularly Steve Rowe and Anne Rowe for being teachers, mentors, and helping me find my first glimpse into another world; George and Mark of The Company of 1415; Andy Cundy for a generous welcome and friendship in Brighton; Mark Walsh for being so different and yet often so much the same; and especially Tom Maxwell, teacher, friend, fellow explorer, light relief (!), recommender of TV series', and now test reader.

Fellow facilitators and learning junkies: Lance Giroux from whom I have learned so much about the Samurai mindset and leadership; Jamie Morgan, soul-brother and fellow mischief-maker; Claire Breeze and Sue Cheshire, corporate fairy-godmothers; Martin Egan who introduced me to Conscious Business; Leanne Lowish and the team at Axialent with whom I continue to explore and deepen with it; Kate Shela teacher, and fierce dancing warrior of the heart; Shianna Ravenlaw for quiet wisdom; Tom Anderson friend, generous support, and the man who got me a 'proper' job!

I have been blessed with many beautiful friends over the years and no few fantastic teachers, for those not mentioned by name here, thank you for your gifts.

I have failed to keep it anything like as brief as I had intended but be thankful, it could have been a lot longer!

# Contents

# Introduction

For as long as I can remember I have loved fantasy fiction. 'Lord of the Rings' was first read to me when I was 6 and my mum told the story that she was really reading it for my older brother, thinking I would be too young to follow so long and complex a story... Until one night, having just read the part where the King of the Horse-Lords has been killed in battle, she finished, stood next to our bunk-beds to tuck us in and say goodnight and found a little sobbing bundle on the top bunk (me) saying "He shouldn't have died!"  I have read that book myself now many times since and thought the same thing every time I have read of that noble man's death.  I've shed a tear more than once as I have journeyed with those companions.

In many ways Tolkein's writing was more of a moral basis for me growing up than any Bible or other book explicitly intended for moral and ethical education.  In some personal reflection work I did on a course over 10 years ago now we were asked to remember what we dreamed of being as a child.  I wasn't sure at all at first but as I sat with it I realised that, rather than the usual Astronaut, Rock-Star, Bus-Driver, or Footballer,  I had dreamed of being a sword-wielding wizard who goes around helping people!  No-wonder perhaps with what I have just told you of my literary environment, however, that became a touch-stone for me on my personal journey. How could I get as close as possible to that child-hood dream while remaining solidly rooted in the 'real world'? How could I learn to be a man I could admire as much as I admired Aragorn when I was a child? How could I learn to be as wise as Gandalf? How could I learn to be courageous in the face of life's challenges and to see the magic in life when it is tough or even boring? How could I find ways to connect deeply with my companions on my personal adventure in the way that the characters do in my favourite works of Fantasy?

These have been the questions I have sought to answer by the way I live my life and the path I have sought to walk. It has been tough, sometimes I have really struggled and I certainly don't think I've 'made it' or am at the end of my journey with these questions. But today I write this as a martial artist (occasionally sword-wielding) working as a facilitator and spiritual counsellor (magical things regularly happen in my presence), who travels to work with groups and individuals to help them be happier, more aware, successful and fulfilled (basically, going around helping people). In so many ways, I am the man I dreamed of being as a child and I feel like the wonderful stories of my favourite Fantasy writers such as J. R. R. Tolkein, Ursula LeGuin, Robin Hobb, J.K. Rowling, George R. R. Martin and so many others, have a lot to do with how I have grown over the years. These books, the television series' and films have been my companions on the path: they have helped me to process my feelings and heal my hurts; they have inspired me to have courage when life has been hard; they have helped me to dream bigger dreams and hold myself to a higher standard.

I think that stories, especially the epic, mythic stories are meant to be more than just entertainment. I believe that the distilled reality of these grand adventures is there to help us grow as human beings, to inspire our spirits and nurture our souls. In the cynical age we live in where every great leader or inspiring individual is peppered with criticism as soon as they stick their head above the parapet of public life, these stories become even more important. Where else are we to find role-models of greatness? Part of what gives me hope is that these mythic stories are growing in popularity. The 'Lord of the Rings' films, and TV series' like 'Buffy the Vampire-Slayer' seem to have opened the door to mainstream culture engaging with Fantasy as a legitimate rather than purely niche genre, and I think that is partly because in our hearts so many of us are crying out for hero's to inspire us. 'Game of Thrones' is the next step in this evolution, and what a fantastic step! (Pun intended).

In my life, while religions, spiritualities, and philosophies of various types have played significant parts in shaping my character, it is the philosophy of the world's Warrior traditions which have informed me the most. Whether it is the Samurai of Japan, Chinese warrior monks, indigenous warrior Shamans from every continent, or the Knights of medieval Europe the ideas, values, and practices of Warriors from around the world have become my passion and my spiritual home.

Having trained originally as an actor I love theatre. Television is often looked on as not being as authentic as stage plays, and not as grand in scope as film, but I think that has changed. Some of the best writing, acting and directing today is, I believe, coming out of the television industry. Game of Thrones is a perfect example of this: awesome actors, fantastic script, amazing production quality and cinematography, all being brought together to tell a truly epic story. I love TV and it is because of programs like this that, that is the case.

So... this book is my way of sharing with you my twin passions: Mythic stories and the Warrior's path. Game of Thrones is so rich with great warriors and noble acts it seems the perfect inspiration for sharing this rich and deeply practical philosophy. While the story is also full of deviousness, betrayal, and underhanded politics it is only against this background that the true nobility can stand out as it should. Without darkness we could never recognise light, and it is one of the most perennial spiritual truths that life is hard. Without challenges to overcome we could have no hero's and if the characters did not face the pain and sadness of life then we wouldn't invest belief in their world or identify with them as people. It wouldn't have true resonance with our own lives. While the darkness is there and I will definitely speak of it, my focus here is on how we can embrace the best that humanity has to offer. It is not that Machiavellian scheming isn't worth understanding – it is, so you don't get caught in the traps people might set for you, or the temptations to become one of the schemers – but it is my experience that what helps me live my life most fully is to grow my capacity for courage and nobility and act as much as I can from that place.

In the words of F.W. Farrar:

*"The true preparation for life, the true basis of a manly character, is not to have been ignorant of evil, but to have known it and avoided it"*

My hope is that for those of you who come to my writing because you love George R. R. Martin's books or the excellent Television series by HBO, that this book will help to deepen your appreciation of the characters in those stories, and that those stories then become a portal for you onto another world – that of the warrior traditions and their attendant philosophies. For those of you who come to this book because you love the warrior traditions, my hope is that it will help to reveal how wonderful stories can teach us a great deal about martial philosophy. I have found that sometimes stories can teach us just as much, or even more than studying the history of our martial arts.

However you come to this book, I hope that it helps you to reflect not just on the rarefied environments of Game of Thrones, and warrior philosophy but on your own life. I believe that stories and philosophy can help us to learn how to live our lives with greater awareness, consciousness, dignity, and grace. I wish you courage, beauty, and joy on this journey, your life.

## A little note on spoilers and bandwagons...

Firstly, I wanted to let you know that I have only drawn on examples of scenes from season 1 of HBO's 'Game of Thrones' series. I wanted to stick to the TV series because that is what will make this book most accessible, to most people. As much as I love George R. R. Martin's books, some people will only ever watch the TV program. I'm OK with that. I'm not a die-hard "read the book or you're a light-weight" fan, and as I have already mentioned, I think it is really good theatre – a great piece of drama. I believe the simple beauty of the philosophy of the warrior's path can enrich anyone's life, and more than anything else, that is what writing is about for me – making the world a better place. Maybe in a small way, but none-the-less. I think the philosophy expressed here and the reflections on the characters and their dilemmas will enhance your experience of all the TV series to come, and indeed of the books too as the themes here are eternal questions of humanity which is part of what I think Martin, and HBO are exploring themselves. However the examples are, as I say, drawn from season 1. What that means in terms of spoilers is that if you have seen all of season 1 then you have nothing to worry about! If not then proceed with caution... I have to give away a certain amount about the plot to use it as the inspiration for my work.

Secondly, I wanted to address directly something which may be on your mind: Am I just jumping on the bandwagon? The short answer is yes and no, but as with most short answers, that doesn't tell you very much! I have definitely seen an opportunity to as my friend calls it "meme-surf" - to ride the wave of popularity around a particular concept, idea, or form. However, when I say "Inspired by..." I mean that. I watched the series and loved the way they brought the world, characters, politics, struggles and dilemmas to life so much it inspired me to want to connect with this great story and become a part of the rich flow of meaning that comes from this kind of genuinely great story-telling. The warrior's path is so strongly a part of this story, and it is so strongly a part of my life that it just felt like it made total sense for me to write this book, and when better than now? I believe the message I offer here, which I pass on from previous generations of truly wise men and women is a powerful message about how we can grow into the fullness of ourselves as human beings and in doing so, make the world around us a better place. I think that is a message of both challenge and hope which we are all in need of sometimes, and there is much in the world right now which needs challenging, and many people who could use a greater sense of hope. I see it as timely in that way too.

Enjoy this book for what it is: an opportunity. Take that how you will...

# The Warrior's Code

## Chapter 1 – The Warrior's Code

*"A hedge night is the truest kind of knight... Other knights serve the lords who keep them, or from whom they hold their lands, but we serve where we will, for men whose causes we believe in. Every knight swears to protect the weak and innocent, but we keep the vow best, I think."* [i]

In every warrior tradition around the world that I have come across there is a code of behaviour which serves as moral foundation and ethical yard-stick for the warriors in that culture. Just as this quote suggests of the knights of Westeros, the land where George R. R. Martin's 'A Song of Ice and Fire' is set, it varies greatly how strictly these codes have been adhered to. However, they were put in place and generally the warriors most respected and admired over the generations have been warriors who serve a higher purpose than their own glory, and a key part of that life of service was abiding by a code of honour.

The vow that Knights take in Westeros is never stated in full in the books that I'm aware of but it is spoken in part in one of Martin's novella's as:

*"...in the name of the Warrior I charge you to be brave... In the name of the Father I charge you to be just... In the name of the Mother I charge you to defend the young and innocent... In the name of the Maid I charge you to protect all women..."* [ii]

I'd guess the rest of the vow continues the pattern and is based on the Seven Gods: Warrior, Father, Mother,

Maid, Smith, Crone, and Stranger. Perhaps only Martin knows for sure! The Night's Watch also swear an oath which I shall explore more in chapter 5 on Duty and Service.

Lord Beric Dondarrion uses a simpler oath in 'A Storm of Swords 1: Steel and Snow' but that feels more like a basic and expedient oath rather than an expression of a code of honour. For completeness' sake, here it is:

*"...do you swear before the eyes of gods and men to defend those who cannot defend themselves, to protect all women and children, to obey your captains, your liege lord, and your king, to fight bravely when needed and do such other tasks as are laid upon you, however hard or humble or dangerous they may be?"*[iii]

The most obvious examples of these codes of behaviour in our history are Chivalry in Europe and Bushido in Japan. The Chivalric Code of Charlemagne was:

*To serve God and defend the Church*
*To serve the liege lord in valour and faith*
*To protect the weak and defenceless*
*To give succour to widows and orphans*
*To refrain from the wanton giving of offence*
*To live by honour and for glory*
*To despise pecuniary reward*
*To fight for the welfare of all*
*To obey those justly in authority*
*To guard the honour of fellow knights*
*To eschew unfairness, meanness and deceit*
*To keep faith*

*At all times to speak the truth*
*To persevere to the end any enterprise begun*
*To respect the honour of women*
*Never to refuse a challenge from an equal*
*Never to turn the back upon a foe* [iv]

Japanese *Bushido*[1] is much harder to pin down in terms of a well defined or specifically recordable code. The main attempt to set out the key principles of Bushido is the book 'Bushido: The Soul of Japan' by Inazo Nitobe written at the end of the nineteenth century and first published in 1900. In the introduction Nitobe himself says that true Bushido defies definition but he is attempting to describe it to help Westerner's to understand the Japanese psyche. The qualities and concepts named in the chapter headings are:

- *Rectitude or Justice*
- *Courage, the spirit of Daring and Bearing*
- *Benevolence, the Feeling of Distress*
- *Politeness*
- *Veracity and Sincerity*
- *Honour*
- *The Duty of Loyalty*
- *Self-Control*
- *The Institutions of Suicide and Redress*
- *The Sword, the Soul of the Samurai*
- *The Training and Position of Woman*[v]
  (This last is more respectful and less sexist than it sounds!)

---

1   *Bushi* = Warrior, and *Do* = Way ---- The Way of the Warrior

This is a helpful framework upon which to hang an initial understanding but in my experience of the Japanese martial arts, I have spent many years diving deeply into what is essentially a living and breathing philosophy of life and still feel like I am discovering new facets all the time. One of the best ways I have found Bushido expressed is in the 'Hagakure'[vi] which is a book than began life as a secret record of an old Samurai's wisdom collected by a younger Samurai of the clan. As such it is made up of a huge collection of short sayings and anecdotes. I have found that by sitting with these and seeking to understand them within the cultural context of ancient Japan, I feel like I get a flavour of what it meant to live your life according to Bushido, and while I have enjoyed and deeply respect Nitobe's work in defining Bushido for outsiders, it is the Hagakure along with practising the physical arts which I feel has given me the greatest insight into true Bushido.

Many contemporary martial arts also have some kind of behavioural code which may express a moral or spiritual philosophy explicitly, but any code of behaviour is an implicit expression of a set of values. Essentially it says "This is what we think is the right way to behave." One example of a code with explicitly moral content is Gichin Funakoshi's Twenty Guiding Principles of Karate:

1.  *Do not forget that Karate-do begins and ends with rei[2]*

2.  *There is no first strike in Karate*

3.  *Karate stands on the side of Justice*

4.  *First know yourself, then know others*

5.  *Mentality over technique*

---

2   *Rei* is Japanese for the formal bow but also translates as 'Respect'

6.  *The mind must be set free*

7.  *Calamity springs from carelessness*

8.  *Karate goes beyond the dojo[3]*

9.  *Karate is a lifelong pursuit*

10. *Apply the way of Karate to all things, therein lies its beauty*

11. *Karate is like boiling water: without heat, it returns to its tepid state*

12. *Do not think of winning. Think, rather, of not losing*

13. *Make adjustments according to your opponent*

14. *The outcome of a battle depends on how one handles emptiness and fullness (weakness and strength)*

15. *Think of the opponents hands and feet as swords*

16. *When you step beyond your own gate, you face a million enemies*

17. *Kamae (ready stance) is for beginners; later, one stands in shizentai (natural stance)*

18. *Perform kata exactly; actual combat is another matter[4]*

19. *Do not forget the employment or withdrawal of power, the extension or contraction of the body, the swift or leisurely application of technique*

20. *Be constantly mindful, diligent, and resourceful in your pursuit of the Way [viii]*

---

3   *Dojo* is the word for a training hall and means 'Place of the Way'
4   *Kata* is the word for the patterns of solo movement that Karate practitioners use to practice their skills

It is no surprise that these have a moral and even spiritual feel to them as Funakoshi was a scholar of oriental philosophy as well as a martial artist. His reference to the 'Way' is the core concept of Taoism, the indigenous spiritual tradition of China and one of the key influences on Zen Buddhism. Tao means 'Way'. It is the way of the universe and your personal path through life. It is the gateway through which the microcosm relates to the macrocosm. If you'd like to understand more about Taoism then you may enjoy my other books[5], however, for now hopefully you can see that Karate's principles have clear directions in terms of how to live a 'good life' and even have a kind of spiritual lineage within the context of which practitioners could deepen their moral foundation.

An example of a more obviously pragmatic code is the Marquess of Queensbury rules (one of the early established sets of formal rules for boxing):

1. *A fair stand-up boxing match, in a twenty-four foot ring.*
2. *No wrestling or clinching.*
3. *Three minute rounds, one minute between rounds.*
4. *Ten seconds to rise and return to the scratch line.*
5. *A man hanging on the ropes in a helpless state is considered down.*
6. *No seconds or any other person allowed in the ring during the rounds.*
7. *If the match is stopped, the referee designates a time and place to continue.*
8. *The gloves must be fair-sized boxing gloves of the best*

---

5   'A little book on finding your Way – Zen and the Art of Doing stuff' and also the forthcoming 'My Tao Te Ching – A Fool's guide to Effing the Ineffable.'

*quality, and new.*

9. *A glove that bursts, or comes off, must be replaced to the referee's satisfaction.*
10. *A man on one knee is considered down, and if struck the other forfeits the match.*
11. *No shoes or boots with springs allowed.*
12. *In all other respects, the match is governed by the revised London Prize Ring rules.* [viii]

While this is mostly concerned with the practicalities of a fight, it still says a lot about the values of those who chose to engage in this warrior art. The word 'fair' is used twice. This is not a word of precise technical definition, it is a word of personal, ethical judgement. If you hit a man while he is down you forfeit the match – this is another expression of fairness and to me speaks of maintaining a level of civility which must be part of your way of life in order for it to be sustainable under the emotionally charged conditions of a fight. Essentially much of this expresses a set of values to do with justice, dignity, respect, courage, and honesty and in that way, while it at first glance looks like a set of rules it is no less a warrior code than Charlemagne's code of Chivalry, or Bushido.

I think all of these warrior codes share something implicitly which has been expressed more explicitly about Bushido: living the code involves a lot more than what is written down. Not only is the code not adhered to as strictly by all those who profess to follow it as by the minority of dedicated followers (the "Truest Knights" of our original quote), but really following the code is much more than the 'letter of the law' so to speak. I believe that in any life path, in any moral code, in any spiritual or religious path for that matter, there is a vast field of implicit, lived experience which goes to make up the code and any written or spoken definition can only ever express a small part of this larger reality. Returning to our example in story, Game of Thrones: at first glance many of the characters seem to be sworn knights, but most of us watching it would only pick out a handful who we'd consider the true knights within the piece. I'd suggest that there are some not-so-obvious candidates as well. Lord Eddard Stark is perhaps one obvious example of a true knight, but his honour proves his downfall. Does that then mean that all honourable men are doomed to be taken advantage of by those less scrupulous than themselves? Tyrion Lannister does not seem much of a knight but many of his acts show clearly a much more knightly sensibility than many others including his brother Jaime who at first glance looks much more in keeping with our expectations of warrior-hood. I think Varys shows many of the deeper features of knighthood and warrior-hood in his commitment to service and care for the greater good. Whether that proves true in the long haul we will find out. Ser Allister who trains the new recruits in the Night's Watch at the wall probably follows the letter of the law of the knights vow religiously, but most of us would recognise that he has about him a quality of presence and lack of grace and respect which marks him out as a poor example of the knight's vow as it should ideally be lived. These are just a few examples of how the Warrior's code shows up in the series and we will explore many more as we start to look at specific qualities within the way of the warrior in future chapters.

Whether you are a martial artist yourself, follow a moral or spiritual teaching tradition or are just considering what the core values are that you want to live your life by, I'd strongly recommend that you keep your eyes and mind open to the subtleties and the undefinable, but highly visible, qualitative aspects of any life path. If you have never considered the principles by which you live your life, it may be something worth thinking about. You will be living out certain value choices unconsciously whether you like it or not so if you want to have some influence over what those values are it is worth your time and energy to ask yourself some tough questions and begin to recognise the values you are embodying now, and the ones which you really want to live by.

Having considered how the Warrior Code turns up both in Westeros and in our own history, and having reflected a little on its relevance in our day-to-day lives, I finally want to turn our attention to why these codes sprang into existence in the first place.

Acknowledging that at the lowest common denominator, 'might is right' why would those most skilled and therefore powerful in the realms of 'might' apply a strict set of rules to themselves? Couldn't they do what they liked? One could argue that the societies these warriors belonged to may have had a hand in creating these kinds of rules to make these fierce individuals safer to have as part of the community – and that's a totally valid point. However, my personal experience, and the anecdotal evidence from the histories of many great warriors I have come across seems to suggest there may be more to it than that - maybe not in every case, but certainly in many. Before I go on I do want to acknowledge that there have definitely been times in history when warriors were not harnessed to these kinds of moral codes. I think this was most frequently the case in societies and environments where basic human needs were not getting met (sustenance, space, shelter) but not exclusively so, and even in the societies and environments where such codes were in place they did not necessarily meet our modern expectations of freedom and justice for all. As mentioned before, it also varied greatly how deeply these codes were adhered to. However, all that said, if instead of looking at the historical specifics we look at the archetypal ideal and the mythological picture I still come back to this question of why those most able to enforce their will on others would chose instead to be in service? I consider there to be a deeper human truth than the purely historical which we can find by examining this mythological view, and as one of my teachers, Simon Buxton quotes his teacher as saying:

*"The only difference between Myths and History is that everything in the Myths is true."* [ix]

In the stories of so many great warriors I have seen a common theme: that they are wild and destructive when young, but once they have proven themselves and begin to mature, their focus shifts from being the most dangerous person, to being the most complete person. In the Chinese martial traditions there is an informal title 'Master of the Five Excellences' which was someone who had mastered not just the martial arts but meditation, healing, composing (music, poetry, painting), and performing (acting, dancing, speaking). This is very like the Western concept of a 'Renaissance Man' – someone who was really a well rounded person who had achieved highly in diverse art forms including the typically manly ones – like sword-fighting, the typically sensitive ones – like dancing or the fine arts, and the academic ones – such as the sciences, medicine, literature or philosophy. These are both expressions of what I am talking about. Another example would be in central America where different levels of spiritual development were signified by a counting system with twenty being the human optimum state. Someone who would be really respected might be spoken of as a 'Twenty' meaning that they are a wise and well developed person who has explored the many different levels of themselves as a human being and understands their place in nature.

In the Samurai era of Japan, particularly later on around the 1600's when the Emperor and the Shogun ruled all of Japan and there was therefore a kind of peace, Samurai warriors were often to be found practising various fine arts. This was not an entirely new thing, but in this time of peace something had to be found to occupy the fierce spirits of these mighty warriors so that they didn't get bored administrating their lands and end up picking fights just for the fun of it! In some ways then, these art forms were contrived methods for keeping the most skilfully violent people in check, but there were many examples where it went much further than this and it is one of those I want to highlight as an example of this progression from death and destruction to growth and even great beauty. Miyamoto Musashi is one of the most famous Samurai of all time, however, he was not born into the Samurai Class (like being a Knight or Lord), and never ruled an estate. He was a *Ronin*[6], which was a kind of Samurai who did not serve a single Lord but was taken into service by Lords when they needed an experienced veteran warrior. This was not a mercenary. Mercenary's were considered to be without honour. Most Ronin took on this role if their Lord died in battle but they had not been dishonoured by it[7]. However, some common-born men who were great fighters managed to be accepted as Ronin just because of their fighting prowess and Musashi was one such man. He won his first duel at the age of 13 fighting an adult Samurai, and went on to win a total of 60 duels before he withdrew from fighting and eventually died. He also fought in several large scale battles over the years in the service of various Samurai *Daimyo*[8]. What is less commonly talked about regarding Musashi is that he was arguably one of the finest brush painters of his generation as well as being a highly skilled calligrapher. It was these arts that he came to focus on as he got older along with recording his philosophy on combat and life in 'The Book of Five Rings.' Even his fighting style shifted away from killing his opponents. This was partly due to his awesome level of skill – the fact that he <u>could</u> defeat opponents without killing them – but I believe it also shows a growth into a particular mindset. Most Samurai fought with a single sword called a Katana (the second shorter sword being kept as back-up and for ritual suicide), but Musashi developed a very rare style of fighting using both swords. In one of his final duels after

6   Translates as 'Wave Man'
7   If they had, they would have committed ritual suicide commonly called *Hara Kiri* but correctly called *Seppuku*
8   This translates most directly as 'Big Man' but was the title of a senior Samurai Leader, like a Lord with sworn knights and vassals

he had taken a position in a Daimyo's household as a teacher to the Lord's son's, Musashi used 2 wooden training swords against an opponent armed with a razor-sharp steel blade and each time his opponent attacked Musashi trapped his sword using the 2 wooden swords thus making it impossible for his opponent to continue attacking. As I say, while this definitely demonstrates a peak of skill in swordsmanship, I think it also signals a shift away from killing which was reflected in the rest of his life at this time.

Another more modern example, also from Japan, would be Morihei Ueshiba, the founder of Aikido. He is famous for his Aikido as being a martial art, but with a peaceful and even loving intent. A core part of the embodied philosophy in this art is to take care of your opponent – even as they are thrown, they are thrown in such a way as to help them land safely. What is less often talked about regarding Ueshiba is that he was much more violent and even war-like when he was younger. He developed and trained a small paramilitary group with whom he invaded a part of China, with the intention of annexing it to form their own country – on a small scale this was war, and people died. Ueshiba talked of having had a profound realization and I can believe it. I think there must have been a massive turning point in his life for the violent youth to have become the heartfelt representative of peace. While Ueshiba's shift is seen as a full-on spiritual transformation, I think this is not so different from the shift that occurred in Musashi and the link between the martial arts and the fine arts, and healing arts is not restricted to Japan. In China many of the finest calligraphers also practised martial arts. Often the local doctor would also be the martial arts instructor. In Europe, many very fine writers and poets in ages past were Knights and military men. The art of ballroom dancing was originally a warrior art: it was a way to demonstrate your grace, elegance, dignity, and general physical prowess off the battle-field, and therefore in an environment more likely to be frequented by ladies!

To me, these links between the arts of war and the arts of beauty and healing are significant when we consider why the mighty would burden themselves with a code of behaviour. I have witnessed it in myself and others, and it is recognised in the field of psychology that a nearness to death will often bring out in us a desire to feel more alive. Whether it is thrill-seeking behaviour, sex, physical exercise, partying, or making big life changes, when those near to us die many of us will find ways to connect more profoundly with life. My suspicion is that in these ancient warrior traditions something similar was going on. At an archetypal level, what this says to me is that life and death walk hand-in-hand. This makes sense to me and is borne out in many philosophies from around the world – a prime example being the concept of yin and yang: opposites are interdependent on each other and one contains the seed of the other. Practically and physically this makes sense too because without death, there can be no life. If plants don't die, other creatures can't live, if those other creatures don't die, then other larger creatures can't live... and so on. Equally, and for the same reasons, it is just as true that destruction and creation go hand-in-hand. Warriors often are, like the ancient God of War, Mars, destroyers. Just as a nearness to death brings out a desire to feel nearer to life, I think a nearness to destruction brings out a desire for a nearness to creation. In this way at a fundamental level I see the warrior arts which are so often inextricably linked to harm, destruction, and ultimately death, must be connected to creative arts which seek to heal, create, and ultimately give life. For these reasons I think that people drawn to a warrior's path (who are not clinically imbalanced such as psychopaths) will eventually find their way to creative and healing arts. It is part of how the healthy human psyche balances itself. To come back to the question of why the mighty would harness themselves to a warrior code, I think it is for similar reasons of balance. Not an imposed balance by a fearful society but a healthy balance born of the wisdom of older warriors initiating the younger warriors into a life not just of destruction and death, but of creation and life too. By binding themselves to a warrior code they moved from practising fighting skills to practising a warrior art. The warrior's very way of life became an art form. They took acts which were often destructive and put those acts in service of a creative and essentially life-affirming purpose in the wider context: service, care, fairness, justice, faith, one of the most beautiful of human traits – courage, and protecting the weak (preserving life). For me it is the code of honour – and living within the spirit of it, not just the letter – which distinguishes the purely martial from the martial art. The Fighter, from the true Warrior. When considering the characters in 'Game of Thrones' this is the key thing to consider. It is a story set in a time of war so many, or even most of the characters are involved in acts which lead to destruction – either directly or by command – but, the key distinction is whether they are doing so for a larger purpose than merely their own self-aggrandisement or desire for revenge. In the larger context, are their actions life-affirming or life-degrading?

Gregor Clegane 'The Mountain' is a very clear example of pure destruction incarnate. There is nothing of the true Warrior about him. But while Loras Tyrell 'The Knight of the Flowers' for example seems much more gallant, I'm not sure there is anything more significant to his motives than his own glory. The distinctions in this realm are not clear-cut and just as in life, true Warriors, truly honourable men and women are rare. As I mentioned before, some of them may not be obvious at first glance. Eddard Stark is so often a clear example of a Warrior's heart, but some of the blindness that leads to his downfall is due to his attachment to a rigid sense of his own honour, which strays at times into pride. His honour is more important to him than the safety of the common-folk. Ironically, Tyrion Lannister's lack of attachment to any sense of honour sometimes means his acts are more honourable. I will speak more of this in Chapter 8 on Honour.

The dedication to a higher purpose that I would suggest comes with a commitment to a true Warrior's path says to me that what we are dealing with here is a spiritual path. That doesn't mean that it needs to have any religious trappings, to be 'woo woo' or 'new-age', it just means that the Warrior's path is more than a job or even a vocation: it's a calling. As such it is a path that can be walked whoever you are and whatever you 'do.' While I have talked mostly here of historic figures who were martial experts, I would say that just as someone can be a fighter without being a Warrior (such as Gregor Clegane, or Bronn), someone can equally be a Warrior without being a fighter (such as Tyrion Lannister, or Varys perhaps). That holds as true in this world as in Westeros so if you choose to temper and hone your heart and mind, to wield your power wisely, to serve a higher purpose (something greater than your own self-interest) and to follow a code of honour – be it a formal one, or your own personal one, then I say you are a Warrior. To quote Richard Strozzi Heckler in his excellent book 'In Search of the Warrior Spirit' which is his diary and reflections from teaching awareness disciplines to the US Army Green Beret's:

*"There is certainly a legacy that distinguishes the warrior from war. The sacred path of the warrior is part of an ancient moral tradition. It includes the Indian warriors Krishna and Arjuna in the Bhagavad-Gita; Homer's hero Odysseus who outwitted his opponents rather than slaying them; the post-sixteenth-century Japanese Samurai who, in his finest hour, administered a peaceful government while still maintaining a personal discipline and integrity through not only the martial arts but the fine arts of calligraphy, flower arranging, and poetry. It includes the American Indians who lived in harmony with the land and who's ritual wars were exercises in bravery rather than slaughter; the Shambhala Warrior of ancient Tibet who applied power virtues to spiritual development; and Carlos Castenada's celebrated warrior shaman Don Juan Matus. These historical and mythical warriors found their strength and integrity by defeating their own inner demons, living in harmony with nature, and serving their fellow man. I... believe that if we embody the virtues of these archetypal warriors we are acting in support of the whole planet instead of constantly fighting external enemies for petty ends."* [x]

It is this kind of Warrior Philosophy which I will continue to explore in these pages. I will use the wonderful characters from 'Game of Thrones' and their acts both beautiful and terrible as illustrations, and link this with both the historical warrior traditions of the world and, as much as possible, everyday life. I have written this book out of a love of this exploration, but I want it to be relevant to your life. So, I will end this chapter with a couple of questions: What do you value? What is your personal honour code?

# Responsibility

# Chapter 2 - Responsibility

*"Ability to respond does not mean ability to succeed. There is no guarantee that what you do will yield what you want. The guarantee is that as long as you are alive and conscious, you can respond to your circumstances in pursuit of your happiness. This power to respond is a defining feature of humanity. Our response-ability is a direct expression of our rationality, our will, and our freedom. Being human is being response-able."*

- Fred Kofman in his book *Conscious Business*[xi]

One of the qualities which I believe most clearly defines someone as a Warrior is responsibility. Whether they wield a sword or not, true responsibility is core to the warrior mindset. That might seem strange for me to say, you may have been expecting something more like courage, or honour, but responsibility is the one for me. I could understand why this might seem odd, especially in the world we live in where responsibility is so often misused. Many times when people say "Responsibility" what they mean is 'blame'. How often have you heard someone say "Who is responsible for this?" and known that what they mean is "Who can I blame?" However, this is not the real meaning of responsibility, it's real meaning can be found by breaking the word down: Respond-ability. It is to do with the ability to respond consciously to what life offers us rather than having a knee-jerk reaction. A wonderful distinction which has helped me to be clearer about this in my own life is made by Fred Kofman in his excellent book 'Conscious Business'. If I say that responsibility is absolute and unconditional then that can seem like I am trying to say that there are no other factors in your life than your own actions, that if you are faced with terrible circumstances then you only have yourself to blame.... and there's that word again! Blame. The word 'responsibility' has become so thoroughly associated with blame it is hard to separate the two any more. The distinction Kofman makes is that we are not responsible <u>for</u> everything, we are responsible <u>in the face of</u> everything in our lives. I cannot be held responsible for the weather, but I am responsible for my choices in the face of bad weather. On a larger and perhaps less abstract scale, I am not responsible for world hunger. I did not cause it. However, once I know that it is happening I am responsible in the face of it. Whether I campaign, travel to feed people, raise money, donate money, donate food, do nothing, or actively contribute to the problem by acting in ways that will drive up the price of food (for instance), once I know about the issue I am accountable for my choices – if I am response-able. If I refuse to be response-able (and that is a choice) then I can paint myself as a helpless victim of circumstance. "I had no choice..."

Ironically Lord Eddard Stark who, once he reaches King's Landing shows himself to be one of the few in the capitol who is working to act responsibly, has a moment of total irresponsibility when he chooses to serve as King Robert's Hand[9]. In discussing it with his wife Lady Catelyn, he says of his becoming the Hand of the King:

---

9   If you are unfamiliar with the terms of this story, 'The King's Hand' is the formal title of the Lord who serves the King as right-hand-man and executor of the King's decisions. Sometimes it is the Hand *making* the decisions too...

*"I have no choice"*

To which she replies:

*"That's what men always say when honour calls. That's what you tell your families, tell yourselves. You do have a choice and you've made it."*[xii]

We can speak more on the matter of honour in that chapter, and certainly in life there are times when it feels like we have no choices, but Lady Catelyn is right. We always have a choice. There may be times when all choices seem equally poor, or even just equally compelling, but we have choice. Responsibility is about owning that choice rather than denying it even when that is difficult or painful. Sometimes we may tell people we have no choice out of a desire to protect their feelings but even then we engage in a dis-empowering deceit and in our hearts we all know it. I may say "I'm sorry I can't come to your birthday party," but that is not really true. I may be sorry, especially in the traditional root meaning of the word of "I feel sorrow," but it is not accurate that I can't come. The truth is that I am prioritising something else. It would be more honest to say "I would love to come to your party, and there is something else that is more important to me that night." That may be a tougher message but it is more true as well. Perhaps you can see from this example how pervasive the lack of true responsibility is in our daily lives. These may seem like trivial things, just some small words, but as I say we all know the truth of this so we are in a constant mode of lying to each other. We habituate ourselves to this deceit and over time we even begin to believe it. By these many small lies I convince myself that I really don't have a choice. I tell myself the story that I 'can't' go to the party. In this way I build an internal dialogue, and through that a perceived reality that is restrictive, limited, and above all, beyond my control. As I have said before, of course there are factors in my life which I don't control but what I do when I say "can't," instead of "don't want to" is put even more things beyond my control. I build a cage for myself and then lock myself inside it. This is the worst kind of imprisonment – the one we build for ourselves. Victor Frankl, psychiatrist, famous author and founder of Logotherapy formed many of the core ideas of his philosophy driven by his experience of being a survivor of a concentration camp in Nazi Germany. He talks about how in the concentration camp he realised that while all of his external freedoms had been taken away, the one freedom that the guards could not take from him was his own response to his situation. No matter what they did, they could not control his internal choices and responses to them as human beings. This depth of internal freedom is rare but it is possible for all of us to access it, and I would say that we erode this internal freedom by increments every time we say "I can't" when we mean "I'm choosing something else."

Just as we erode our relationship with ourselves through these moments where we deny our response-ability, so too we damage our relationships with others. This is what we see in this exchange between Ned Stark and Lady Catelyn, and where normally she might accept his denial of his own power as a small and socially acceptable lie, here she is too distraught from the injury of her son and challenges him on it. I wonder how different this conversation would have been if he had owned his responsibility and declared his choice – no less painful perhaps, but more honest at least and maybe less damaging to their relationship. I think this is an expression of a deeper pattern of attitude, thought and behaviour for Ned Stark because he has such a strong sense of responsibility about so much. I would say one of his flaws is that he abdicates responsibility when it comes to matters of honour and duty. He reverts to unconscious, knee-jerk reactions based on a very rigid idea of how the world 'should be' rather than how the world really is. This rigidity of mindset is part of his downfall. As we look at this matter of responsibility you are probably seeing that it takes a very high level of awareness to be truly responsible. It's tough! To notice when you are denying your own capacity to choose, to spot it when you are telling a friend or partner a small, convenient lie, to know and acknowledge when your priorities are different than someone else would like them to be, or even to realise when you are acting from an old pattern rather than a live relationship to the world around you. All of this takes a lot of commitment and mindfulness. A wonderful illustration of this is an old story of the great Japanese sword master Tesshu:

> *Tesshu had several students studying with him to master the sword. The best of them was walking down the street in the centre of town one day and as he walked past a horse, the horse startled and kicked. Tesshu's student was so fast and skilful that he managed to deflect the horses kick. Everyone nearby could see that a less skilled man would have been badly hurt or even killed. Of course, the story of this young swordsman's skill spread very quickly through the town,*

*but to everyone's great surprise, two days later he had been dismissed from Tesshu's school of swordsmanship. When one of the town-folk got up the courage to ask Tesshu why such a promising student had been dismissed he said of the incident with the horse "The student had clearly failed to learn what I had to teach." This seemed utterly bizarre to the town-folk and though they pressed him to explain what he meant, Tesshu would say no more on the matter.*

*So... the town-folk cooked up a plan to see if they could catch Tesshu out. Surely he could do no better than the young student in the same situation, what more could a man do? If there was some magic Tesshu could work, they all wanted to see it! Tesshu walked the same route from his home to his school every day. It was always the same, so it was not hard for the locals to find a particularly irritable horse and tie it up outside one of the shops on Tesshu's route. They then all went about their business, surreptitiously keeping an eye out for Tesshu to come past. A little while later at just his usual time Tesshu was walking the way he always walked. As he approached the horse, everyone watched with baited breath... but just before Tesshu got to where the horse was tied up, he crossed the street and walked by on the other side!*

I would say that Tesshu dismissed his student for a lack of responsibility. His knee-jerk reaction showed amazing skill, but he lacked the awareness required to be able to respond effectively to the world around him. What if the horse had been injured or had got more distressed and hurt someone else? That said, Tesshu was a master and it's important to remember that we are all human-beings and while we can aspire to the highest of standards we will all slip sometimes – I suspect even Tesshu had moments where he stumbled on the path!

One of the very clear instances where Ned Stark shows his strong sense of responsibility is right at the beginning where he is beheading a deserter from the Night's Watch. He says:

*"The man who passes a sentence should swing the sword."*[xiii]

In this he is a true leader taking a very hard decision but he takes full responsibility for his decision and bears the consequences of it. He must take a man's life, rather than have someone else do it for him. One of the other negative outcomes of avoiding taking full responsibility for our choices is that we can psychologically distance ourselves from them. It becomes easier to make choices which we know in our hearts are not honourable choices, or even morally congruent choices when we can distance ourselves from the outcomes. In a wonderful talk, economist and researcher Dan Ariely[10] talks about how this shows up in a small way. Some of his research has been to look at honesty and dishonesty and how we apply our moral code. In the example he describes they were getting people to do a task for the experiment and then report their own scores, the higher the score, the more they got paid for taking part. They had university students as test subjects and found that the reported average was higher than the measured average (so clearly people were exaggerating their scores – lying!), but when they got people to promise on the honour code of the university that they were being honest the reported results became more accurate – even though that university has no honour code! What this tells me is that when people are connected to their sense of

_____
10  From this talk on TED "Our Buggy Moral Code"

values, they act with more integrity. Without the reminder of the honour-code, they could 'fudge' it in their heads. They could say to themselves "well, it's about right" or "it's only a little bit..." Once they were connected with the reality that if they 'stretched the truth' they were breaking with their own sense of integrity, they got more honest – with themselves and others. In a larger way, it is part of the dialogue around the warrior's path in the modern military that it is much less clear how to be a true warrior in modern times than in history. When you have to stand toe-to-toe with someone and fight for your life then your courage is not in question, but when you can shoot them from two kilometres away, or press a button and end hundreds or even thousands of lives it becomes abstract. How much do you really have to live with the consequences of your actions? And therefore, how carefully do you consider your choices before you act? Ned Stark deliberately keeps himself face-to-face with the choices he makes and in doing so, I would say that he holds himself to a higher standard and will think much more carefully before he sentences a man to die.

I think it is one of the great challenges of our time to keep ourselves face-to-face with the consequences of our choices because that is part of what will help us to make good choices and to take responsibility for the choices we make. We live in an increasingly remote world where communications happen over vast distances and decisions in one country can affect the entire world. I think the world of business in particular should take note of the lesson Ned Stark offers here: it is too easy for the signing of one contract by some people in a office to create or axe hundreds of job, to preserve or destroy entire habitats, to make or break economies, in simple terms to nourish or destroy life. I think if all executives and politicians made themselves come face-to-face with the consequences of their decisions, we might have better decision-makers, and better outcomes for everyone.

As I mentioned near the beginning of this chapter while we are certainly not responsible for everything that happens in our lives, we are responsible *in the face of* everything that happens. One wonderful example of someone taking responsibility in this way is Ser Barristan Selmy, Lord Commander of the King's Guard. Ser Barristan is a great example of the true expression of many warrior virtues, but the specific moment I am talking about here is when Ser Huw of the Vale is killed by Ser Gregor 'The Mountain' Clegane in the Hand's tourney. Ned Stark goes to see Ser Huw's body and finds Barristan there and asks:

*"Does Ser Huw have any family in the Capitol?"*

To which Barristan replies:

*"No, I stood vigil for him myself last night. He had no-one else."*[xiv]

It is not Barristan's fault the young man is dead, nor is Ser Huw his responsibility as family, but in the face of this tragedy Barristan chooses to do what he sees as his spiritual duty. Knowing there is no-one else, Barristan steps in and answers the perennial question of activism:

*"If not you then who?"*[11]

---

11 Anonymous quote to the best of my knowledge. Part of a larger

It is all too easy to feel helpless when faced with life's challenges. It is hard to constantly turn to ourselves and challenge the voice that says "There's nothing I can/could do..." But if we don't challenge that voice at every step, if we don't do battle with our own apathy and sense of defeat then by increments we die. Perhaps not physically – although the depths of psychological despair can be very directly connected to illness, even terminal illness[12] – but in our hearts we numb ourselves so as not to have to face the deep knowledge that we have given up on life and forsworn our power to effect change. This is a hard road to walk, that is why I see it as part of what makes a person a warrior, but if I want to be able to embrace life fully, if I want to be able to look at myself in the mirror and feel proud of the man I see there then it is a necessary challenge to face.

Viktor Frankl wrote that in the concentration camps people died two deaths. There was the physical death which came when they were killed, but way before that there was a spiritual death as they succumbed to the hopelessness and had the internal freedom I mentioned earlier, the ability to respond (response-ability) beaten out of them. For me, one of the great tragedies of modern life is that while many of us (especially in the so-called 'First-World' countries) have amazing freedoms in so many ways, I see so many people who seem to have given up on this

_____

question "If not now then when? If not you then who?"

12 There is the obvious connection between depression and suicide but also less obviously there have been studies done which connect what psychologists refer to as 'learned helplessness' as a mindset and an increase in the instances of developing cancer later on in life. Ref. - paper "Positive Image, Positive Action" by David Cooperrider.

most essential of freedoms: the freedom to manage and challenge my own response to life's difficulties. I think that our culture of possession where for so many people self-esteem and self-respect is based on how much stuff you own, is at least partly the cause of this (although it is a little chicken-and-egg). When 'Having' is more important than 'Being' it's easy to get drawn into a striving for perceived material freedom (to have anything I want to have) rather than focusing on personal freedom (to be anything I want to be). This same cultural trend is prevalent in much of the world of Westeros as well, where so much can be bought by gold – even, in many cases, a man's honour. Barristan and Ned Stark are two examples of people for whom that is not the case. Tyrion exhibits a lot of personal freedom too in this way. Jon Snow also shows a huge reserve of personal integrity and response-ability. There are others, but they are rare, and most of them slip up at some point. As I say, this is a tough path to walk - I fully acknowledge that and I'm not trying to pretend I'm writing this as someone who is perfect and always standing in my full power, holding responsibility as deeply as I'd like. All I feel I can do is keep working at it to become constantly more aware and constantly more response-able.

Many spiritual philosophies from around the world acknowledge the innate difficulty of leading a good life. One of Buddha's four noble truths is most commonly translated as "Life is suffering." Kung-fu has at it's heart a similar philosophy which resonates for me. 'Kung-Fu' can be translated a number of different ways some of which make fairly obvious sense, such as 'Skilful Movement' but one of the less obvious ones is 'Time and Hard Work.' It is this second translation which I find most useful. While learning to be skilful in your movements will take time and hard work, at another layer this translation speaks to me of just what I have been describing about the path of responsibility: a responsible life takes time and is hard work! That may not seem like a very positive message, but the beauty of it is that if I can accept that life is hard work, that it is often difficult and that suffering is an unavoidable aspect of existence, then ironically, the hard work, the difficulty, the suffering sort of disappears. It's not that these things are any less true of the circumstances of my life but if I accept the reality of the difficulty I don't struggle with it in the same way any more. This is the most profound level of responsibility. It is my struggle against the challenges in life that create my discomfort. If I take really full ownership of my responses then life is only hard, difficult, or full of suffering because I judge it to be. Stuff happens. Life is not a giant persecutor trying to inflict pain, God is not a great big bully in the sky. Stuff happens. And my judgement of it as hard or easy; joyful or difficult; pleasure or suffering is my first response. Stuff happens, I make a judgement about it, I take action upon it. If I can deeply, deeply accept that some of what life offers me will be challenging then I don't need to judge it in the same way. I create my own suffering, life just hands me experiences. Carlos Casteneda, in writing about the path of a warrior shaman, puts it like this:

*"Only as a warrior can one withstand the path of knowledge* (or path of responsibility). *A warrior cannot complain or regret anything. His life is an endless challenge, and challenges cannot possibly be good or bad. Challenges are simply challenges."*

There is no question that what life hands people is different. I cannot even begin to conceive what it was like for Viktor Frankl living through his time in a concentration camp, nor do I ever want to experience such horrors. I have no idea if I would be able to live this philosophy were I to face such a challenge. However, Viktor Frankl's dignity in the face of such a terrible life experience gives me hope that we all have the potential to transcend our circumstances and embrace our deepest human freedom: response-ability. As Aldous Huxley said:

*"Experience is not what happens to a man; it is what a man does with what happens to him."*

King Robert Baratheon has failed to embrace his responsibility. I can have compassion for him as a man who lost his love, and has found himself as King of a nation he is ill-equipped to rule. He was fortunate to have Jon Arryn at his side for so many years, but in another way perhaps that helped him to continue to shirk his true responsibility. It is Roberts' irresponsibility which has landed the realm of the Seven Kingdoms in so much debt – he refuses to face the realities of their finances. This kind deliberate blindness is probably not unfamiliar to many of us. Lots of people today have lots of debt – our increasing debt/credit culture around finance contributed to the financial crash of recent years. Just like Robert Baratheon we were encouraged to it by the social norms and trusted advisor's who said "it'll be ok..." but we still have to bear responsibility for it. With Robert Baratheon, this is one of many ways he constantly seeks to avoid dealing with the realities of his life. There is a scene, after Ned Stark has been struck down by Jaime Lannister and his men, when Queen Cersei is making accusations of Ned and his wife Lady Catelyn (because Cat has arrested Tyrion Lannister, Cersei's brother), and eventually says to Robert that she should wear the armour and he the gown. He hits her and she says:

*"I shall wear this like a badge of honour"*

To which Robert replies:

*"Wear it in silence or I'll honour you again."*

When Cersei then leaves Robert clearly regrets his actions and says:

*"See what she does to me? My loving wife..."*

This is the crux of it. For all her taunts, viciousness, manipulation and resentment, for all of the pain that is so much a part of Robert and Cersei's relationship, she didn't make Robert hit her. He did that. However skilled a manipulator Cersei may be show does not control Robert, and more than this, his statement for me epitomises Robert's relationship to his life. In his head he had to go to war because mad King Aerys killed Lyanna Stark - the woman he loved, he had to take the throne because he had the best claim, he had to marry Cersei because Jon Arryn said it was the right thing to do... and now he had to hit Cersei because she drove him to it. In his mind, none of it is his responsibility. On the flip-side we have Daenerys Targaryen who was an exile before she was born, has been sold like a prize heifer by her own brother to a brute of a man who doesn't even speak her language and nightly takes her in what is pretty much rape. Out of this she manages to build a life for herself, to create a loving and in many ways equal relationship with her husband, to become a Queen (Khaleesi) of sorts, and to win the love of her new people. Daenerys is such a fine example of responsibility in action, it is hard for me not to wonder if perhaps she would make a better ruler for the Seven Kingdoms than the others who are competing for the crown. I'm not looking to demonize Robert here, I can understand how such a thing could happen in a man so thoroughly bred on violence, filled with frustration and stuck in a marriage so full of pain and bitterness, but it does serve us here as a valuable illustration of how easy it is to relinquish our own power – to disavow our ability to respond.

All of the above said, I make no judgement of you as you face your life and it's unique challenges, and I would encourage you not to judge others, as we can never truly know another person's pain or joy, regardless of their apparent advantage or disadvantage. Tyrion Lannister offers Jon Snow a very similar lesson when Jon first begins his training having arrived at The Wall. In Episode 3 we see Jon fighting and beating the other men who have arrived to serve on The Wall with him. They are all criminals of one stripe or another and he has judged them and so much of the Night's Watch as beneath him. He is disappointed to find a collection of criminals where he expected to find men of honour, and in every fighting practice session he takes his disappointment and frustration out on those he trains with. They all resent him. Tyrion, in one of his moments of wisdom, responsibility and care, tells Jon Snow of the histories of the men he has arrived with. Many of them, though considered criminals, only came to be that way because life dealt them ill fortune. Often they have displeased someone in power who has then abused that power in having them convicted. Once Jon hears this, he is open and humble enough to take responsibility for his circumstances, to change his attitude, and begins to work to make the world around him a better place rather than remaining a victim and imposing his misery on whoever he comes into contact with. In this Jon makes what I call 'The Warrior's Choice'.

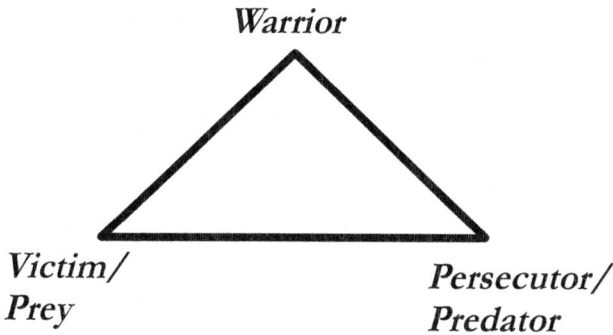

## *The Warrior's Choice:*

**Warrior**

**Victim/
Prey**

**Persecutor/
Predator**

All too often in life we polarise our choices. We think it all has to be either black or white, right or wrong, good or bad. This happens unconsciously in so much that we do, and it happens in power dynamics as well. Many people who feel victimized – by a person or just by life's circumstances, consciously or unconsciously – will think that the way out is to become a persecutor. Few people would recognise it in those terms consciously, but what might be easier to recognise is a mindset that says "If you don't want to be the prey, become a predator."

Sadly, if you choose to be a predator, others have to be prey, that's the way it works and whether you mean to or not, while you're trying to free yourself from fear, you become the object of others people's fear. That is what happened to Jon Snow in this example. He felt the victim of fate and, that life had played a cruel trick on him, and in taking our his frustrations on his fellow trainees he became a predator. With a sword in his hand on the practise ground he could beat people up and feel powerful. It was a salve for his wounds. I would say that Ser Alister Thorne's bullying of the young men he was supposed to be training is something very similar – a wounded man trying to erase his wounds by making those around him suffer. As the Persian poet Rumi put it:

*"People of the world don't look at themselves, and so they blame one another."*

What Tyrion helped Jon to do was look at himself, and see that he was fighting the wrong enemy. These other men were to be his sworn brothers, and Jon's circumstances were not their fault. Moreover, he was only making his circumstances worse by making enemies of the very men who must one day watch his back. Jon's life was only going to consist of time served on The Wall and dog-hard work (a bitter dose of Kung-Fu). As long as he was caught up in resenting this, he was incapable of doing anything to improve the situation. Once Tyrion helped him get a hold of himself and start taking responsibility in the face of the cards that life had dealt him, Jon was able to start working to help those around him and make his own little patch of the world a slightly better place. He could,

*"Shine one corner of the world"*[xv]

As the Zen Master Shunryu Suzuki put it. This is the Warrior's Choice: to refuse to be either victim or persecutor, predator or prey. I believe there is always a kind of magical third option in any situation. Life is rarely only black or white, and Tyrion helped Jon to see that and act responsibly.

The final aspect of responsibility I want to explore is how we can end up punishing ourselves out of a misguided sense of responsibility. What we are really doing is blaming ourselves and as I discussed at the beginning of the chapter, true responsibility has nothing to do with blame. The irony is that in this kind of self-blame we actually limit our capacity for true responsibility because our pain will cloud our judgement and probably inhibit our awareness. The example of this from 'Game of Thrones' is when Arya Stark is speaking to her father Lord Eddard Stark (Ned) and says that it is her fault that Mycah (the butchers boy) is dead. This is off the back of Mycah having been killed by Sandor 'The Hound' Clegane because Prince Joffrey has accused Mycah and Arya of attacking him when in truth, he was trying to bully them and fight them with a steel sword when they had been playing with sticks.[xvi] It is one of the first instances where Prince Joffery is shown to be quite as monstrous in his arrogance and viciousness as we come to see is his modus operandi.

Arya is faced with a terrible situation and the fact that she wishes to take responsibility for Mycah's death is, in my judgement, a noble wish. But it is misplaced as Ned tries to help her to see. Arya is not responsible for Mycah's death, she is responsible in the face of it. She is responsible for her behaviour towards Joffrey, and perhaps there was another or a better way of diffusing the situation when it originally happened, I don't know. It would be easy to judge and blame Sansa for not coming forwards with the truth of the situation and backing up Arya's story, but as I've said before, responsibility is not about apportioning blame and as Ned Stark points out, Sansa is in a very difficult situation as she is betrothed to Joffrey. As it turns out, just the fact that she has seen him shamed is enough to have turned him against her but she was not to know that. As I will discuss in the chapter on Duty and Service, sometimes we are 'in service' to many different masters (or values) and when they clash and emotions are running high it can be hard to find our centre and make conscious choices about our priorities. For that matter, by the time Sansa is brought forward I think Mycah has already been killed. Many people could be held partially responsible (or held accountable) for Mycah's death – Joffrey, King Robert, Queen Cersei, The Hound, very probably other Knights and Guardsmen – but that is not the key message here. The thing I am most wanted to explore here is that Arya is not responsible *for* his death, she is responsible *in the face of* his death. She makes the classic error of those of us who are prone to taking the weight of the world on our shoulders (and no wonder, I find it hard to manage this in myself and I have over 20 years experience on her!), that of blaming ourselves. As I have said, not only is it not accurate, it is also debilitating – it stops us doing the real work of responsibility. The blame game, whether we turn on others or turn on ourselves will only cause more pain, it never heals.   That is why this distinction around responsibility which Fred Kofman has made so concisely is so important:   We are unconditionally responsible in the face of our circumstances, we are not necessarily responsible for what life brings us in the first place. If we wish to be true Warriors then we must get a hold of this distinction and live it as fully as possible, otherwise we will constantly be compromised in our capacity to respond consciously to our environment. Our energy will be tied up with blaming – either ourselves or others. Responsibility requires great awareness and no small amount of courage, but it is the gateway to our greatest power.

# Self
# Knowledge

# Chapter 3 - Self-Knowledge

*"Let me give you a some advice, bastard: Never forget what you are. The rest of the world will not. Wear it like armour and it can never be used to hurt you."*

*- Tyrion Lannister speaking to Jon Snow*[xvii]

Self Knowledge or self-awareness is the foundation stone of everything else I will talk about in these pages. In truth all of these warrior virtues is completely interdependent upon all of the others. It is very hard to be one of these things without embodying the others – as I said in the last chapter, it is very hard to be truly responsible without a high level of awareness. I'd also say that once one of your principles slides, the others are likely disappearing with it. This is the meaning of the phrase:

*"The road to hell is paved with good intentions"*

You can have the best intentions in the world but unless your actions consistently follow those intentions then even a small slip in one area can undermine all of your principles frighteningly quickly. If you slip, you need to get back on track fast, and if you don't have sufficient self-awareness then you can be making slips left, right, and centre and never notice it. Pretty soon, you're in a hell of your own making! In the scene I have quoted at the start of this chapter Tyrion Lannister opens the door for Jon Snow to be much more honest with himself and thereby, much more self-aware. Tyrion Lannister is a great example of the power of self-knowledge as he makes such great use of the gifts he does have and manages his weaknesses well most of the time although his temper and sharp tongue run away from him a fair bit! I will speak more of how Tyrion uses his gifts in the chapter on Honour. For this section I want to focus more on how Tyrion helps Jon Snow to foster his own growing self-knowledge. In the scene I have quoted from above, Jon is ashamed of his illegitimate birth, and understandably so in the world he lives in. In Westeros many people will make all kinds of assumptions about your character just because you are born outside of wedlock and much closer to home, Ned Stark carries a great deal of shame about his infidelity no matter how committed he is to raising Jon as his own Son. Lady Catelyn Stark clearly and fiercely resents Jon's presence. While I can completely understand why Jon would want to deny and reject his origins his suppression of this aspect of himself doesn't stop it playing out in his consciousness and his life, Tyrion is right: there is no getting away from what you are. As Carl Jung said:

*"Until we make the unconscious conscious, it will rule our lives and we will call it fate"*

I believe this is true socially as well as personally. Whether Jon owns his illegitimacy or not it's impact on his life is the same. He can go on feeling like the victim of his birth or he can embrace his circumstances and make the most of who he is. At least if he embraces being a bastard he can be who he is and live his own life rather than trying to be another Robb Stark with a starting handicap. This is connected with what I was discussing in the last chapter about accepting that life is suffering. Jon has had a tough start to life in some ways (very blessed in others). His pain is created by his rejection of his own nature. What Tyrion is pointing out is that if he embraces the facts of his life then they cannot be used to harm him. There is an old Native American teaching about thanking people who upset you which I first came across in one of Jamie Sams' books:

> *You should thank those who upset you because they have shown you where you are hurting yourself. We may hear a hundred potentially hurtful things a day but most we just shrug off as not being true, or embrace because we are happy with those qualities in ourselves. The one or two that hurt and stay with us for days or even years are the ones where someone has echoed a criticism we have already levelled at ourselves. In this way, those who hurt us have opened the door to us healing our relationship with ourselves.*

For me this goes a step further than what Tyrion says because rather than needing to armour yourself with your perceived flaws, once you have owned them and healed your relationship with this aspect of yourself then they aren't flaws any more. Syrio Forel, Arya's sword teacher and a master swordsman in the tradition of the Water-Dancers of Bravos teaches something similar to Arya:

*"Syrio says every hurt is a lesson, and every lesson makes you better"*[xviii]

Obviously Syrio is referring to physical lessons in swordsmanship, but this is another way that I see the path of the warrior turning up in everyday life. How can you take every hurt you receive and instead of letting it harm you further by brooding on it or seeking revenge, use it as a lesson in self-knowledge and an aid in healing your relationship with yourself?  In this way you become a warrior in every day of your life, a warrior of your own emotions and psyche.

Although her strength of character often gets her into trouble, Arya Stark does know herself well – it is one of her strengths and I would say it is part of why she does feel responsible for Mycah's death (as discussed in the last chapter), because she reflects deeply on what she's done and how her actions have affected others.  There is a wonderful, though slightly sad moment where she is speaking to her father Ned Stark about what the future holds for her, and he says:

*"You will marry a high lord and rule his castle, and your sons shall be knights and princes and lords."*

To which Arya replies:

*"No, that's not me."*[xix]

Anyone who has been paying attention can see she is right!  Even as young as she is, she knows who she is.  There is another sweet moment, full of pathos when Ned Stark says:

*"War was easier than daughters."*[xx]

Ned Stark is a man that in many ways knows himself well.  I think it is because he knows his flaws as a father, because he knows that he struggles with it, that he makes such a good father. In this way self-knowledge has the potential to enable us to become skilful at what we are not gifted at. If I don't know that I am unskilled at something then I have no opportunity to improve at it. I'd suggest that Ned's weak points are most pronounced around the places where he is unconscious of his weakness. When he knows he is not good at something and can admit it he is willing to do the hard work to improve. When he is just plain unconscious of a flaw, of course, he can do nothing about it. One example of such a flaw is his honour. He is so rigid about his own sense of honour that he finds it very hard to live with the fact of his failures in living to his own standards. He won't talk about Jon Snow's mother, he gets upset at being reminded of his infidelity and is clearly very hard on himself about it as King Robert observes on the road to King's Landing. As James Baldwin once said:

*"Not everything that is faced can be changed. But nothing can be changed until it is faced."*

Ned is so active in suppressing the flaws in his own honour that it blinds him to the flaws of others as well. He makes unreasonable, superhuman demands on himself, and unconsciously expects more of other people in terms of honourable behaviour than they are ever likely to give. In many ways it is this more than anything else that proves his undoing: he expects Lord Littlefinger and the Gold-cloaks to do as they say they will, and Cersei and the court to respect Robert's dying wishes. His unconscious assumptions about honour and trust leave him open to betrayal. Once again, the truth of Jung's perspective is borne out:

*"Knowing your own darkness is the best method for dealing with the darknesses of other people."*

In Ned Stark's case his unwillingness to really face his own darkness means he is blind to the darkness in others. Terminally blind as it works out. A conversation between Petyr Baelish and Roz, the whore from Winterfell who travels to King's Landing speaks directly to this point:

Ros says:
*"What she don't know won't hurt her."*

To which Petyr replies:
*"A stupid saying. What we don't know is usually what gets us killed."*[xxi]

For Ned Stark, this is true both of what he doesn't know about others and his environment, and what he doesn't know about himself.

Samwell Tarly, like Arya Stark is a good example of self-knowledge. He knows he is a coward. In the context that I am writing about warrior philosophy, that may seem a strange quality to use as a good example! However, as I've talked about with Ned Stark, if you don't know something, you can't deal with it. Because Sam knows he is a coward, he can face that and deal with it. He struggles profoundly in dealing with his cowardice in the field of combat – of course he does – but there are other ways to be brave and skilful than with a sword and fortunately Jon Snow, Maester

Aemon, and Lord Commander Mormont are wise enough to see this. Sam gets given a job that makes use of his gifts. As well as helping others to see him for who and what he is, Sam's open acknowledgement of his own cowardice also gives him a kind of strength. While there are many ways that Ser Allister Thorne and some of the new recruits in the Night's Watch can torment Sam, calling him "Coward" is not one of them. Just as I described in the example from Native American philosophy, because Sam owns his cowardice, no-one can harm him with it. There is a way that, whatever his gifts and flaws, Sam is who he is, and I can admire him for that.

As Chogyam Trungpa says:

*"The key to warriorship... is not being afraid of who you are. Ultimately, that is the definition of bravery: not being afraid of yourself."*[xxii]

By this definition, I would say that Sam is very brave. He knows himself and he is not afraid of himself. I will say more about Sam's particular brand of courage in the next chapter on that subject, but for now I just want to emphasise that he knows and faces the realities of his own character and that in itself is to be admired – that is one version of being a warrior, no matter how you fare in a fight against an outer opponent. You have faced the inner opponent and sometimes that is the harder task, as we see in the example of Ned Stark's failure to confront his own darkness.

This idea of facing your own 'inner opponents' before turning to face the outer ones is spoken of very directly in The Hagakure – one of the classics of the Way of the Samurai:

*"Narutomi Hyogo said, "What is called winning is defeating one's allies. Defeating one's allies is defeating oneself, and defeating oneself is vigorously overcoming one's own body.*

*It is as though a man were in the midst of ten thousand allies but not a one were following him. If one hasn't previously mastered his mind and body, he will not defeat the enemy."*[xxiii]

The men who's thoughts and philosophies were recorded in this book were fiercely practical men of action. This was not based on an idea of what winning took but on concrete experience of going into battle and single combat and testing themselves. If they are saying that facing the inner battle and knowing yourself is what counts, then I think that is worth listening to!

One of the twenty principles of Karate which I referenced in chapter 1 also speaks to me of the need to face your own 'inner opponents' before facing the outer ones:

*"First know yourself, then know others"*

I think what Gichin Funakoshi was getting at when he set this as one of his twenty principles is that we see the world through filters. None of us really sees the world as it is. At a basic biological level, we receive information about the world through a set of organs and senses which are necessarily limited. Just by existing we are bombarded by so much raw data that if we could perceive it all we could never process it all and our brains would be overloaded in even the attempt. So our sensory organs are tuned in to certain ranges or frequencies of data which are most vital to our functioning. Even just those ranges of data are overwhelmingly large and complex, so after we receive this limited bandwidth of information, it is further filtered, edited and digested within our brain and a tiny portion of it is presented to our conscious minds for use in choosing our actions. As you can probably see, that's a lot of filtering! So much is disregarded or suppressed. That limited range of data is filtered further by our psychological state in that moment. An example of this might be:

*You are walking through a quiet part of town and it is quite late at night. As you pass a shop window you notice a beautifully carved chair which is just the thing you have been looking for as a reading chair. The shop is closed as it's late, but you start looking to see if you can see a price on the chair, a phone number for the shop so you can call first thing in the morning to ask them to hold it, and an opening time so you can come back and buy it.*

*All of a sudden you hear a loud bang! It sounds like a gunshot. Your heart races and you start looking for the source of the sound, listening to see if you can hear someone nearby, looking for different ways to head back home, your mind flashing through all the ways you might run to safety...Is that someone in the shadows across the street...?*

*There is another bang. This time the sky lights up and you realise that they are fireworks! By the gold and green light of the 'rocket' you see that there is no-one across the street just a plant growing up the side of the building. You feel relived and almost like laughing – how silly to be so scared! Taking a breath of the night air you can smell a bonfire maybe a couple of streets over, and you can hear some faint cheers for the firework display. You see another launch into the sky and decide to stand and watch a bit. Blue and red falling stars scatter across the sky... It's a beautiful night...*

In each paragraph of this example your focus would be entirely different. Once you notice the chair, everything else disappears and you tune out your environment. With the perceived gunshot, the chair is forgotten and your environment is swiftly assessed based on the limited criteria of possible danger, and possible escape. With the firework realisation the shop and even the streets are soon forgotten as you look to the skies. We are constantly filtering the data we receive about our environment based on what seems important in the moment and much of the rest will be lost to our conscious awareness. There is a famous experiment about this in which a video was made where 2 groups of people, one lot in white, one lot in black, are passing basket balls[13]. For the experiment people were asked to count how many times the basketball is passed between the people in white. Plenty of people get that right. What the majority of people miss is the fact that a guy in a monkey suit walks through the group throwing basket balls, beats his chest and then walks out the other side of the shot. The amazing thing is that the majority of people taking part in the experiment, when asked if they saw the gorilla, had missed it entirely! The typical response was: "What Gorilla?!" The participants in the study had got so focused on the task of counting the passes of the ball that they tuned out everything else. We

---

13 Chabris and Simons – you can find the video on Youtube and
they wrote a book called 'The Invisible Gorilla'

selectively filter, tune in to and tune out so much. *What* we filter will be determined not only by our biology but by our psychological state (survival in the gun example, attention with the chair in the shop – or the gorilla!), our beliefs and our values. If I believe the world to be a beautiful place then I will tend to notice that which is beautiful, if I believe it is ugly, I will notice the ugliness. That doesn't mean that I am completely in control of my world and if I don't notice danger, then it can't harm me – that's delusional narcissism! However, the world in our awareness is amazingly variable, and far less concrete than most people imagine. If I am always on the lookout for danger, I am likely to find it. Where one person sees a potential criminal hiding in his hooded sweatshirt, someone else might see a guy trying to keep his ears warm on a windy day. What the truth is for the guy in the hood may be something else again.

How this all applies in a martial environment is that if you don't have some awareness of what you tend to filter out, then you may be missing important information. If I have an unconscious belief that women are not as good in a fight as men (which, I hasten to add, I don't – I've known some fearsome women!) then I could underestimate a dangerous female opponent. If however, I increase my self-knowledge and realise that I have this prejudice then while I may still disregard women at first glance, there is a chance at least that I will check myself and reassess the situation. If I don't know myself then it will do me little good finding out about my opponent. However I assess them will pass through my many filters and unless I have some knowledge of what those filters are (particularly beliefs and values) then I will dismiss much of the useful information I have gathered.

This all applies just as much in daily life as it does in a martial context. Without cultivating self-knowledge, I could be ignoring potential opportunities left, right and centre. I could be misjudging my friends, misunderstanding my family, passing over business opportunities because I have an unconscious belief that I could never achieve something like that, and just plain missing the beautiful moments in life because I have dismissed it as irrelevant data. All of this could be going on unconsciously, my entire life could be being run by my habitual ways of thinking. Free Will is a result of self-knowledge: You are only as free as you are aware. To quote Jim Morrison:

*"The most important kind of freedom is to be what you really are. You trade in your reality for a role. You trade in your sense for an act. You give up your ability to feel, and in exchange, put on a mask. There can't be any large-scale revolution until there's a personal revolution, on an individual level. It's got to happen inside first. You can take away a man's political freedom and you won't hurt him-unless you take away his freedom to feel. That can destroy him. That kind of freedom can't be granted. Nobody can win it for you."*

By now you are probably seeing how vital an internal awareness is to living the Warrior's Path, and how self-awareness is key if you are to stay on that Path with any consistency. For the final part of this chapter I want to look briefly at how you can bring the discipline of self-knowledge to noticing the ways and the places that your internal world, leaks into the external world. In the Hagakure, it says:

*"A warrior should not say something fainthearted even casually. He should set his mind to this beforehand. Even in trifling matters the depths of one's heart can be seen."* [xxiv]

At first glance this could look like a paranoid statement about not allowing yourself to be seen as cowardly. I read it differently, and I think the second sentence is the key:

*"Even in trifling matters the depths of one's heart can be seen."*

In our smallest acts, our deepest beliefs and values will still be visible. In order to really live consciously, with awareness, and with real self-knowledge we must be dedicated to the task and willing to keep challenging ourselves. It is easy to get a bit more aware, to notice a pattern of behaviour and think "Now I've got it! I won't do that again..." But in my experience it is rarely that simple. I feel like every time I catch myself in a pattern I'm not happy with, the pattern gets smaller. The good news is that as it is smaller then it is less damaging when I next slip up. The bad news is that, as it is smaller, it takes even more attention to spot the pattern before I have slipped and done something I am not happy about. It is said that learning Tai Chi is first done in Feet, then Inches, then Half-Inches, then Quarters, and so on. I think the journey to self-knowledge is the same. If you stick with it, then you can refine the quality of your presence a lot but things also get more complex, and require even more attention to detail as you go. Once you begin down this path I'm not sure there is an end point, I can't promise you you'll ever be in a position to say "OK, I'm done now, I can relax." As Dan

Millman's classic character 'Socrates' says of the path of self-knowledge:

*"Better never begin, but once begun, better finish."*[xxv]

The moment that brings all this to mind for me in Game of Thrones is when Lady Catelyn has realised that her Son Bran's fall from the tower was no accident, after a man is sent to murder him in his bed. She gathers her son Robb, Theon Greyjoy, the master at arms Ser Rodrick, and Maester Luwin in the Godswood to share her suspicions and fears. She says that she believes the Lannisters are involved and Robb says:

*"They come into our home, and try to murder my brother! If it's war they want..."*

Theon cuts in with:

*"If it comes to that you know I'll stand behind you."*

And Maester Luwin rebukes them:

*"What? Is there going to be a battle in the Godswood?! Huh? Too easily words of war become acts of war. We don't know the truth yet."*[xxvi]

This scene wonderfully contrasts the impetuous, and often blind actions of youth with the measured wisdom of Maester Luwin. Unlike some of the Maesters we meet Luwin seems to be a very practical man as well as an educated one, and a thoughtful one. In this scene for me he shows his real value as an advisor in taking a strong stance and challenging people's assumptions. The other characters are ready to jump on any piece of information, any excuse to surge into action and it is Maester Luwin who takes the more measured response. His words echo the previous quote from the Hagakure, particularly the phrase:

*"Too easily words of war become acts of war"*

As I was describing earlier with the example of the shop and the gunshot which becomes a firework display, our beliefs and values act as filters on our perceptions and all too often we see what we want to see. In this phrase, Maester Luwin voices the danger of such filters. From jumping to conclusions, we can jump to actions and they may be actions we regret. Just because they are right that the Lannisters are involved, doesn't mean they have the whole picture as we find out later when Lady Catelyn accuses and arrests Tyrion Lannister who, while he may be many things, is quite probably innocent in the matter of Bran's injury and attempted murder. Just as I was describing with what is said in the Hagakure, Maester Luwin recognises that even in our smallest acts, even in the words we use, our subconscious habits of thought and deed can be seen. While Robb acquits himself well in many ways on the battlefield when the time comes, there is no doubting that at this moment in the story he is a young man who has grown up fighting, dreams of glory, and explodes at any perceived insult or threat to the honour of his house. He is no politician and is not thinking clearly. He is to a great degree blinded by his anger – and understandably so. We all have moments where our upset or outrage blocks our capacity for clear and reasoned thinking. When we perceive a threat, it can trigger a response which is often referred to as "Fight or Flight." This is an instinctual response which is biologically hard-wired and is very useful if you are faced with combating wild-animals (as we were regularly in ancient pre-history when our brains were evolving). There are a bunch of physiological responses which are triggered in the body when we go into "Fight or Flight" whereby 'non-essential systems' are closed down and other systems ramped up. However, the assessment of what is 'non-essential' is based on the kind of threats we faced a very long time ago – such as fighting and escaping lions! The digestive system and immune systems are suppressed, blood thickens, hormones are released – many amazing and quite dramatic changes in the body's functioning. If you want to understand more about all these responses I will be looking at that in detail in my forthcoming book on 'Somatic Presence', but what is key here is that one such change is that chemicals are released in the brain which inhibit access to higher brain functioning (the Human fore-brain which is the seat of reasoned thinking). When people get upset, angry, or stressed and say "I just wasn't thinking clearly..." that is literally, physiologically true. Robb Stark has perceived a threat to his brothers life and to his family dignity. That is all very real for him so in this moment he is blinded not only by his beliefs and pre-conceptions about the Lannisters, but by his emotions (his anger), and even by his physiology (perceived threat triggers "Fight of Flight"). He is really not seeing things very clearly! In this he is very fortunate to have Maester Luwin at his side to rein him in. Perhaps things would have gone very differently in the story if Lady Catelyn had, had Maester Luwin with her when she met and arrested Tyrion Lannister in the tavern on the road from King's Landing. Maybe Ned would have had time and opportunity to finish his investigations and to have brought evidence before King Robert. Even with more years and perhaps more wisdom than her son, Lady Catelyn is blinded by her anger, fear, assumptions and possibly even some of the culturally normal beliefs about the character of people who are disfigured which seem to be commonplace in Westeros.

It is my experience that with greater self-knowledge, we can learn to notice when we have been triggered into "Fight or Flight", or when we are being run by our emotions, or when one of our unconscious beliefs or assumptions is driving our behaviour. My suggestion is that when we cultivate sufficient self-knowledge we can have an 'inner Maester Luwin', perhaps like an angel on our shoulders, who can help us notice when we have been hooked into one of our habitual patterns of thought or behaviour. When we are aware enough to notice these hooks, we have a chance to reclaim our free will from our unconscious urges and act in accordance with our deepest sense of truth and justice, rather than from knee-jerk reactions and primal instincts. In this way we can become warriors who are not only courageous and fierce, but dignified and compassionate as well.

# True
# Courage

# Chapter 4 – True Courage

*"The key to warriorship... is not being afraid of who you are. Ultimately, that is the definition of bravery: not being afraid of yourself." - Chogyam Trungpa*

You may recognise this quote from the last chapter, and as I said there, by this definition, I would say that Samwell Tarly is very brave. He knows himself and he is not afraid of himself. Sam may seem a strange figure to use as a positive example in a book on the warrior's path, and doubly so in a chapter on courage: he is a self-confessed coward after-all! However, I think he demonstrates a much more subtle kind of courage which begins with his willingness to know himself and not be afraid of his own nature, but goes further than that in the way he is willing to own and face his own nature publicly. He is not afraid of others seeing his fearfulness and he has an almost child-like innocence which seems to be indestructible even in the face of his father's scorn, abuse and rejection, and similar treatment from so many of the others that he meets. As I see it, Sam doesn't fear his own nature and that is rare, and though he may frequently be afraid of how the world around him might harm or challenge him, as another great man once said:

*"Courage is not the absence of fear, but rather the judgement that something else is more important than fear." - Ambrose Redmoon*

As a side note, there is a great moment when some of the more obviously warrior like characters acknowledge that courage does not entail the absence of fear. Robb Stark has just given the command to call the banners so he can ride to war and he's sat with Theon Greyjoy. Theon has a rare moment of wisdom:

Theon:
*"Are you afraid?"*

*Robb holds up his hand and it's shaking*

Robb:
*"I must be."*

Theon:
*"Good"*

Robb:
*"Why is that good?"*

Theon:
*"It means you're not stupid."*[xxvii]

To return to Sam as an example, while there are many times that he struggles to face his fear and make the choice that something else is more important (as in the Redmoon quote), there are also many times where he faces his fear and does stand for what he believes in. Even just in joining the Night's Watch, in turning up in the practice ground each day, in keeping trying to make friends with people. He keeps offering his friendship to Jon and the others vulnerably and with an open-heart. Whether that is wise or not is another conversation, but in my judgement, it does show a particular kind of courage. To quote the writer Erica Jong:

*"Many people today believe that cynicism requires courage. Actually, cynicism is the height of cowardice. It is innocence and open-heartedness that requires the true courage - however often we are hurt as a result of it."* [xxviii]

I see Sam's persistent innocence as the kind of courage Erica Jong is talking about here. In an environment like the Night's Watch and with the personal history Sam has had with his father, I think his preservation of an open-heart is doubly courageous. I also think it is the source of a more obvious kind of courage such as that which Ambrose Redmoon refers to: making something more important than fear. Sam places friendship, his care for others, and his sense of doing what's right before his fear for himself on a number of occasions. One such occasion is when Jon hears of his father's execution as a traitor and leaves the Wall in the middle of the night to go and join his half-brother Robb in waging war and avenging their father. Sam leaving could cost him his life too – this is no small action – but Sam leaves anyway to go after Jon to remind him of his oath and bring him back to the Night's Watch. Sam risks his life for the life of a friend. That is not the action of a coward. Sam is a deeply fearful person and he is no-one's idea of a fighter, but perhaps he had just not found anything in his life before this point which was important enough to him for him to face his fear and act anyway. It's a wonderful moment in the story, and there is a sadness for me as I wonder what Sam's life could have been like if he had, had a father who was willing to accept him as he is – a scholar - rather than trying to force him to be a fighter. I wonder how Sam's father, Lord Tarly's fear played a part in the way he treated Sam. What was Lord Tarly so afraid of that he could not make his love for his son more important than it? What was he afraid of in Sam (or in himself to go back to Trungpa's perspective) that he felt the need to beat it out of Sam and eventually send him to the end of the known world? Of the two of them, who is the real coward? I have no definite answers, but I think they are interesting and important questions especially for those of us who are parents. Can you be courageous enough to love your child no matter what?

Part of what I am addressing in Sam's example is that there are different kinds of courage, and that whether an act is courageous depends on the person taking it. It requires little courage for Jon Snow to turn up in the practice yard and fight with training weapons, whereas for Sam, even getting out of bed at the Wall probably takes a feat of courage. To quote Mary Anne Radmacher:

*"Courage doesn't always roar. Sometimes courage is the little voice at the end of the day that says I'll try again tomorrow."*

Benjen Stark has a moment with Tyrion Lannister when he speaks to this very point. Tyrion, in a moment which is common for him in terms of acerbic wit, but less common in terms of lack of insight, is needling Benjen Stark about being fearful of what lies beyond the Wall and saying it's only a handful wildlings. Benjen says:

*"...it's not the wildlings giving me sleepless nights. You've never been north of the Wall, so don't tell me what's out there."*[xxix]

In this Benjen is speaking of a literal, physical location which Tyrion has never seen, but the reality is that no-one can see the world through your eyes, and we all have wildernesses within our souls which none but us can ever face. What is easy for me, may be terrifying for you or someone else. What you do without thinking may be someone else's greatest challenge. At the end of the day, only you can truly judge whether you have acted with courage or cowardice. Can you look at yourself in the mirror and admire the person you see there?

While Tyrion is dismissive in his conversation with Benjen, there are other moments I have mentioned where he shows real wisdom, and I would say there are some instances of real courage too. To live as a dwarf in a culture where dwarf children are often left in the woods to die after birth is no small thing. Just to hold his head high takes courage. But he has moments of displaying more active courage too. One such is when he slaps Joffrey. The prince is saying he won't go and give his condolences to the Stark's after Bran has 'fallen' from the tower. Tyrion tells him in no uncertain terms to go and do it and to do so with humility and care. Arguably Tyrion is just doing this to ensure they keep up appearances, but I have the sense from his manner in this scene that it has more to do with his belief that is the right thing to do. Joffrey is vengeful and will be more powerful than Tyrion in the not-too-distant future, yet Tyrion repeatedly ignores the danger to himself in this to teach Joffrey important lessons. This is a situation

Tyrion finds himself in at other times: speaking up and standing up for what he believes to be right, even when it is not the wisest thing for him to do. In fact this habit gets him into very deep trouble more than once. Standing outside the situations, we, as the audience may not always agree with Tyrion's criteria for what to make a stand for but he shows courage in making his stand.

Someone very different to Tyrion, but similar in this matter of standing for what he believes in, is Ned Stark. Sometimes as I have mentioned it is at least partly sponsored by a kind of blind adherence to protecting his honour, and it is certainly one of the factors which contributes to his undoing and eventual death. However, I still consider Ned's stubborn commitment to being true to himself to be an admirable quality and a sure sign of his courageous nature. In a general way Ned refuses to adopt the tends and behaviours of other lords which he doesn't agree with. This is often in contrast to southern lords, and most markedly the lords in King's Landing. Ned knows that his courage is something which only he needs to know. He doesn't need to prove it to anyone else (unlike his honour which he seems to be constantly defending, a sure sign of insecurity). Where many, if not most lords and knights fight in tourneys to prove their worth, Ned doesn't feel the need to, as he tells Jaime Lannister:

*"I don't fight in tournaments because when I fight a man for real I don't want him to know what I can do."*[xxx]

This could seem like paranoia, but it is simple, practical wisdom. In the Japanese martial tradition there is a practice called 'masking your Wa.' This always sounds a little funny to me – just the way the phrase sounds(!) - but it is a serious matter. Your 'Wa' is your power. It is to do with ensuring that your true power is always unknown so that anyone who wishes to challenge you will be 'fighting blind' with no idea what you are capable of or where your strengths and weaknesses lie. Ned is not interested in admiration or showmanship, he is interested in doing things right, and in doing the right things. That's a hard line to walk in a world so predicated on appearance and reputation, and takes courage to stick to it. What I would say Ned is perhaps more guilty of than Tyrion Lannister, is being attached to his own point of view and in being so, he loses perspective. As Winston Churchill said:

*"Courage is what it takes to stand up and speak; courage is also what it takes to sit down and listen."*

As I have touched on before, Ned fails to really 'listen' to his environment and his deafness leads to his downfall.

Ned's bastard son, Jon Snow shows another kind of courage when he says goodbye to is half-brother Bran when Jon is leaving to join the Night's Watch[xxxi]. Bran is in bed in a coma and Lady Catelyn has not left his bedside since the fall happened. Jon has stayed away knowing that Lady Catelyn resents his presence in her home and his closeness to her children. I can understand her resentment of Jon as a living, breathing proof of Ned's infidelity, but it is a harsh reality for Jon to have grown up with when he has done nothing wrong. In this scene Lady Catelyn is overwrought, probably having barely slept for days and afraid for her son's life. On is determined to say goodbye to Bran though and goes to face Lady Catelyn so he can do so. Her hostility towards Jo is palpable in the scene, but he gently asserts himself and walks over to speak to Bran, to say goodbye and wish him a swift recovery. Part of what I admire about Jon in this moment is how contained he is. There is no doubt that he will have his moment to say goodbye to Bran, but he doesn't do it defiantly or aggressively. Even after years of coldness from Lady Catelyn Jon is respectful and even gentle in how he takes his space – but he does take his space. There is a quality which is spoken of in Iaido[14] called 'Kigurai.' If you look this up in a Japanese/English dictionary you will find it means 'Arrogance', but in the context of the martial arts it has another layer of meaning which relates to Jon's demeanour in this scene. What it can also mean is something like self-possession. There is no direct English translation I have found but this is the closest I can get. An example of Kigurai could be that a great master of the martial arts may welcome you and all his guests into his Dojo[15], he may do so with deep grace and utter humility... but it is still *his* Dojo! It has to do with how he owns the space – not out of territorial-ism or because he has anything to prove, but just because it is his place – a simple reality. In the scene I have just described between Jon Snow and Lady Catelyn I think Jon exhibits wonderful Kigurai. He is not looking to prove anything but he will no-longer hide away either. He is just there because that is where he needs to be. He does what he needs to do and

---

14 Iaido is one of the Japanese sword arts, generally considered to be the art of drawing the sword.
15 Means 'Place of the Way' and is the name for a martial arts training hall

leaves.  Jon doesn't exhibit this all the time but it is definitely a quality which is in him and grows in him when he goes to join the Night's Watch.  It is part of what makes him a leader amongst his other brothers-in-training.  It takes courage to exhibit Kigurai.  You have to have the courage of your convictions firmly in hand, and you have to be willing to make a stand for what you believe in to have Kigurai.  One way I consider Kigurai is as the quality of someone living courageously all the time.  We tend to think of courage as something that happens in moments, in response to a challenge, so maybe Kigurai is the quality of presence which occurs when someone embodies courage in an extended moment – and at it's best, in every moment.

While courage can so often be a subtle thing and is hard to judge from outside the person acting, there are clear examples of a lack of courage, especially with the framing we have set up here.  Two characters who I'd say consider themselves courageous, but who's actions for me, fall short are Prince Joffrey and Queen Cersei.  Prince Joffrey falls short of warriorship in so many ways and is almost a living, breathing example of how not to live!  He's an extreme character for whom it is hard to have compassion, between his bullying and shaming of people, lying and breaking his word, and ordering murder just to placate his own ego.  Queen Cersei however, while still fairly clearly set up as the 'Wicked Queen' archetype, is a more complex and subtle character, especially with scenes like the one she shares with Lady Catelyn, where she speaks of losing her first child - King Robert's son.  She definitely has moments of pathos and sympathy.  The scene which clearly shows the lack of courage I'm speaking of is where Joffrey is talking about what he would do if he were King an how he would raise a standing army and crush the North. Queen Cersei begins by asking some wise and well-placed questions in terms of showing Joffrey the flaws in his thinking, going on to say:

*"A good King knows when to save his strength. And when to destroy his enemies."*

To which Joffrey replies:

*"So you agree? The Starks are enemies."*

And Cersei says:

*"Everyone who isn't us is an enemy."*[xxxii]

It is this last phrase which concerns me most. There is no question that Cersei is in many ways a product of her upbringing and her environment, and while I can find some understanding and compassion for the pain and disappointment she has faced in her life, in teaching her son this kind of mindset and belief she is acting counter to everything I have set out so far as defining courage. Her own unconscious vindictiveness goes unexamined, her actions are driven almost entirely by fear, she rarely makes a stand for anything but manipulates constantly in the background, and cynicism is her default attitude and the perceived truth she uses to justify her dishonesty and malice. In this she completely abdicates her responsibility, showing an attitude of 'everyone else is dishonest, the world is broken, I have no choice but to be as dishonest and broken as the rest.' It is this irresponsibility which shows a lack of courage. It takes courage to look at a broken world and chose to face it with dignity. It takes courage to see other people's dishonesty and chose to be honest anyway. No-one can control your actions, you have always made a choice. Just the same, you cannot exercise complete control over your environment: you're not a god, you have to work with what fate, and the people's actions around you, hand you. Cersei not only abdicates this kind of responsibility, but teaches the same paranoid viciousness to her son. Is it any wonder Joffrey ends up a monster? This seems to me both terrible and very sad.

This links us back to responsibility, again showing how all of these values and principles are interconnected. This quote from the Hagakure expresses it elegantly and profoundly:

*"No matter what it is, there is nothing that cannot be done. If one manifests the determination, he can move heaven and earth as he pleases. But because man is pluckless, he cannot set his mind to it. Moving heaven and earth without putting forth effort is simply a matter of concentration."[xxxiii]*

Every single person is awesomely powerful in their capacity to influence the world around them. You are awesomely powerful! The question for all of us is: Do I have the strength of character to embrace my awesomeness?!Courage is a choice just like everything else. You know where the real challenges lie for you and you will know if you have faced them. There are many factors that can knock us off track or make it hard to listen to the voice of our conscience, but at the end of the day we have to make the hard choice to make a stand for what we believe in and we have to keep making that choice again, and again, and again.  As I spoke about when describing the quality of 'Kigurai', courage is not really about a single decision in the face of overwhelming odds.  That shows the capacity for True Courage, and I don't want to make light of great achievements, but I think True Courage only really shows up in the grind of day-to-day life.  Can you keep your centre and stand for what you believe in, even in the face of the tiny assaults of daily life?  The real threat to our integrity is rarely from one monumental event that could smash us to pieces, it is from the chip-chip-chipping erosion of our willpower by the pressures of the ordinary.  As William Butler Yeats put it:

*"Why should we honour those that die upon the field of battle?  A man may show as reckless courage in entering into the abyss of himself."*

I don't know that I'd put it quite so strongly – I wouldn't want to underestimate the sacrifice of someone who gives their life for their cause.  However, many if not most of the people reading this book will not be soldiers, or be facing physical threat on a daily basis, but that doesn't mean we cannot show courage, or embody a warrior mindset.  Indeed, as I say, in some ways I think the stamina we need to face just our everyday struggles over and over again can be the greater challenge.  Do you have the courage to 'enter into the abyss of yourself' and face the reality of who you are?  Having done so, do you have the courage to admit to yourself where you are falling short of the man or woman that you dream of being?  And then, do you have the pluck to take a hold of yourself and move heaven and earth to make the best of the life that you have?

To borrow from Carlos Casteneda:

*"To be a warrior is not a simple matter of wishing to be one. It is rather an endless struggle that will go on to the very last moment of our lives. Nobody is born a warrior, in exactly the same way that nobody is born an average man. We make ourselves into one or the other."*

At it's heart, the choice to be courageous and turn towards the challenges you face in your life <u>is</u> what makes you a warrior or not. Once again I will say that all of these values I am exploring in chapters of this book are interdependent. I don't believe you can really have one without the other and as we are exploring them I hope that is becoming clear for you too. That said, I can see what Samuel Johnson meant when he wrote:

*"Courage is reckoned the greatest of all virtues; because, unless a man has that virtue, he has no security for preserving any other."*

# Duty
# &
# Service

# Chapter 5 – Duty and Service

*"Hear my words, and bear witness to my vow: Night gathers, and now my watch begins. It shall not end until my death. I shall take no wife, hold no lands, father no children. I shall wear no crowns and win no glory. I shall live and die at my post. I am the sword in the darkness. I am the watcher on the walls. I am the fire that burns against cold, the light that brings the dawn, the horn that wakes the sleepers, the shield that guards the realms of men. I pledge my life and honour to the Night's Watch, for this night and all the nights to come."*

*- The Oath sworn by the Brotherhood of the Night's Watch*[xxxiv]

There is much mention of duty in Game of Thrones and talk of 'who you serve' in terms of your liege lord, as in any feudal society. The rigid hierarchy of such a culture means that there is great clarity about who you are working in service of – at least officially. But who and what you are really working in service of is not so simple as whom you swear allegiance to. We are all acting in service of many masters at any given moment – that is as true in Westeros as it is in our world and in every day of our lives. In this moment, as I sit here writing, I am in service to: myself - my standards and reputation, also taking care of my health and welfare, my wife and son to provide a income for our family and consider their needs when I'm working, you as reader to write something worth reading, society to offer a perspective that contributes to the greater good, George R. R. Martin and HBO to treat their work with respect, perhaps my ancestors to not blight the family name (!), and at subtle levels others too. This is even clearer and yet more complex when I am doing other work for an employer where I can add them, my colleagues (in terms of caring for their professional reputation), and the client(s) to the list as well. Sometimes the many things we are in service of clash and we have to prioritise. I may work late and compromise my health for the sake of the work and earning a living for instance. Ned Stark struggles with many levels of service when he chooses to take the role of King's Hand: service to Robert as his closest friend and almost family, service to Catelyn and his children, service to the people of Winterfell and the North, service to the Realm, service to his own honour, service in so many directions and many of them in conflict.

In the world of Westeros, it is the Night's Watch who are most profoundly in service to the greater good, that is why I have begun this chapter with their oath. The other two main order's which people dedicate themselves to for life are the Kingsguard and the Maesters. The Kingsguard are in service to the King, and the Maesters primarily serve whoever they are sent to. It is the Night's Watch who truly serve all, and they have a strong foundation in the warrior path too. They also very explicitly forswear most of the other things which a person may be in service of: love, family, personal honour, regional affiliation, political connections, possessions, and rewards. Their service, at least in the terms of their oath, is pure. There are times in my life, when my multiple senses of duty seem to be at war with one another, that I could easily wish for such a clear sense of purpose. Because that is part of what service is about: purpose. Having a very clear sense of purpose can be hugely reassuring, I think that may be part of why some people choose to serve in the armed forces, and I think that is perhaps why Jon Snow goes to serve in the Night's Watch. As a bastard Jon doesn't know where he fits. He is neither of true noble birth nor entirely of the common-folk, he is with the Starks but not part of the family, he is brought up by his father but not truly welcome in his home, he doesn't really belong anywhere. For any of us desiring a sense of belonging it is easier to embrace a ready-made reason for being than to discover our own. I think that is at least part of what Jon is doing by heading for the Wall: seeking a place to belong. That is why it is so disappointing for him when he finds it manned by cut-throats and thieves rather than noble men, and that is why, when he accepts it for what it is he becomes a leader amongst the recruits. He aligns himself completely with the purpose and mission of the Night's Watch and in that becomes a beacon of clarity for the other men. He steps powerfully into a sense of belonging, and for a bunch of other young men lost in the world, his friendship offers them a doorway to belonging too. I think that often why young men find their ways to either the more outspoken religious or political groups, or for that matter to martial arts Dojo's is because they want more than anything a sense of belonging and purpose. These kinds of environments with their clear moral codes, boundaries around behaviour, causes to support, and groups of other seekers to join and feel a part of, give access to a ready-made and clearly defined purpose and a group to belong to. The Night's Watch is the perfect place for men to find such belonging with it's own uniform, isolated location, the Wall as an inspiring symbol of that purpose, strict rules about behaviour, and a clear sense of an enemy in the form of everything the other side of the Wall!  Maester Aemon expresses this clarity when he says to Tyrion Lannister:

*"The Night's Watch is the only thing standing between the realm and what lies beyond."*[xxxv]

This kind of clarity of purpose, while being alluring in its own right also helps you to be more focused, present and therefore more effective.  That is why it is sought after in organisations and has been for hundreds of years.  King Robert Baratheon speaks very eloquently about the value of such unified purpose when he is talking to Cersei about the danger posed by Khal Drogo and his Dothraki horde should they ever make it across the sea to the Seven Kingdoms:

*"One army, a real army united behind one leader with one purpose. Our purpose died with the Mad King.  Now we've got as many armies as there are men with gold in their purse and everybody wants something different."*[xxxvi]

Again we can see in what King Robert says why one clear and simple purpose to surrender ourselves to can be so attractive.  What once took the form of a motto in the coat of arms of a noble house, today finds form as the mission statement of a company.  The family 'words' in Westeros are slightly more ambiguous but serve a similar function.  Syrio Forel when teaching Arya Stark gives a great example of the way split concerns, or to put it another way, being in service to multiple things disrupts your effectiveness.  Arya is worried about her father and

Syrio says:

*"You are not here.  You are with your trouble.  If you are with your trouble when fighting happens...*

He disarms and trips her over,

*"More trouble for you!"*

He then goes on to say:

*"How can you be quick as a snake or quiet as a shadow when you are somewhere else?"*[xxxvii]

There is no question that serving many masters can rob us of our clarity of mind and action.  That is why some priests and monks adopt such simple lives and chose not to have families.  As a still relatively new father, I am sharply aware of how having a child has given me both a strong sense of purpose, and a far more complex set of priorities.  If I am not clear about how I am prioritising in a given situation I can end up procrastinating endlessly, so being clear about what I am working in service of is important if I am to be as powerful as I can be.

One group of warriors in history who had a very strong sense of service are the Samurai of medieval Japan.  In fact, 'Samurai' can be translated as meaning 'one who serves.'  To some degree the Knights of medieval Europe had a strong sense of service in the clarity of a feudal, hierarchical culture and the Divine Right of Kings (which meant that Kings were chosen by God and their actions were therefore unquestionable), but they did not have the total commitment of the Samurai. We can see an example of this in a story from the Hagakure:

*"Once when Lord Katsushige was hunting at Nishime, for some reason he got very angry. He drew his sword from his obi (belt), scabbard and all, and began beating Soejima Zennojo with it, but his hand slipped and his sword fell into a ravine. Zennojo, in order to stay with the sword, tumbled down into the ravine and picked it up. This done, he stuck the sword in his lapel, crawled up the precipice, and just as he was, offered the sword to his master. In terms of quick-mindedness and reserve this was matchless resource."[xxxviii]*

If you had any doubts about your sense of service to your lord you would not throw yourself into a ravine just to retrieve his sword, especially after he dropped it while hitting you with it! This is being offered as an example of the perfect behaviour, but to many of us it will seem crazy. Some context which might help is that, similarly to Europe's Divine Right of Kings but even stronger, the Emperor of Japan was considered to be an embodiment of the Gods in earthly form. A Lord who served the Emperor was therefore quite literally acting on behalf of the God's so serving your Lord was seen as direct service to a higher purpose. In this context perhaps it makes more sense. I think most of us want to be in service to a higher purpose and in a survey conducted by Roffey Park[16] it was found that what a large group of people working in office environments most wanted from their work was a sense of purpose, and what they felt was most missing from their work was a sense of connection to a larger purpose (I'm paraphrasing but this was the gist of it). A higher purpose

---

16 A leadership institute in Sussex, UK.

doesn't have to mean anything religious, new-age, or weird, it can be 'the greater good', or something to do with your social conscience, or the future of your children – as well as possibly being connected to a larger spiritual purpose. Really it's just about being in service to something more than your own ego, much as I was discussing in Chapter 1 around following a Code. If you truly believe that you are acting in service of the greater good, you may be willing to do extreme things, indeed, police officers, fire-fighters, soldiers and many other people around the globe take extreme actions often at risk to their lives out of a sense of service.

So that gives a fair picture of the gifts that being in service can give us, but there are shadows of Service and Duty as well. The first is the shadow of fanaticism. Just as people will do extraordinarily wonderful and nobles things in the name of the greater good, people will do terrible things and cite the same justification and sense of service to a higher power. Nazism was in theory about creating the best version of the human-race possible, and fundamentalist terrorists of all backgrounds, faiths, and politics kill many innocent people apparently in service to a higher purpose. Westeros is not short of examples of the same. Much is done 'in the name of the King', or the Crown, or the Throne, or the Realm which is terrible and has much more to do with personal agendas and power struggles. At one point, when he's in the Dungeons, Ned asks Varys:

*"Tell me Lord Varys, who do you truly serve?"*

*"The Realm, my Lord. Someone must."*[xxxix]

That may be true in his perception, he does seem to have his own personal sense of honour and justice, but whether all that he does is sanction-able, even if he truly does intend to serve the Realm is another matter. One example of this, even when he's not following his own mysterious agenda, is when King Robert orders Daenerys Targaryen assassinated. Ned Stark makes a stand against it as there is only a small risk in his judgement that Daenerys' marriage and pregnancy to Khal Drogo poses a threat to King Roberts rule. Ironically it is the assassination attempt which eventually galvanises Khal Drogo to action to invade the Seven Kingdoms. Both Varys and Grand Maester Pycelle argue for the Killing of Daenerys:

Varys:
*"I understand your misgivings my Lord, truly I do. It is a terrible thing we must consider, a vile thing. Yet we who presume to rule must sometimes do vile things for the good of the realm..."*

Pycelle:
*"I bear this girl no ill will but should the Dothraki invade how many innocents will die? How many towns will burn? Is it not wiser, kinder even, that she should die now so that tens of thousands should live?"*[xl]

While both points potentially have merit, and most would see the wisdom of one person dying so that thousands of other can live, their conclusions are based on speculation and there is no guarantee that Daenerys' death will buy the peace they desire. Once again we see Varys' championing of the service of the Realm, and we see Pycelle's roots in an orientation to healing (though how much that guides his actions when we meet him is questionable). This is a sticky and complex issue, not least of all because the people around the table are not unified by being in service to the same master: be it crown, realm, king, people, honour, or selfish profit.

Another shadow-aspect of Service and Duty is the personal cost of it. It can be a weighty responsibility to truly serve, and to fulfil your duty. Anyone who has been in service where lives are on the line can tell you that. Even the less extreme, more day-to-day sense of service of a parent juggling providing for the family, with spending time with that family can be a tough burden. To quote Robert Jordan:

*"Duty is as heavy as a mountain, death light as a feather."*[xli]

I think Robb Stark feels the burden of his duty a great deal as we head into the second part of the series of Game of Thrones. There is a clear moment where this shift begins to happen, when Ned has been attacked by Jaime Lannister and Stark men have been killed. He and Theon Greyjoy are talking about it and Theon says:
*"It is your duty to represent your house when your father can't"*

*To which Robb replies:*

*"And it's not your duty because it's not your house."*[xlii]

This comes across from Robb as a dismissal, and Theon, ever spiky about such things takes it that way. But I think something else is going on for Robb. He is feeling the full weight of his Duty, and where Theon sees a glorious and righteous march against an enemy, Robb has more of a sense of the potential enormity of taking up arms and calling the banners. This is not the first time Robb has come face-to face with the weight of his growing duties, indeed, by this point he has been wrestling with it for some time. There is a beautifully played and very sad scene where Lady Catelyn has been sat beside Bran, who is still unconscious after his fall, for days and is ignoring and rejecting her duties of running Winterfell. Robb has started to pick these up already and steps in at this moment to say that he will resolve the issues that Maester Luwin has brought to Lady Catelyn. Robb challenges her though – and that is no small thing to challenge your mother! She is understandably distraught, but her emotion has blinded her. She thinks she is in service to her son by sitting by his bedside night and day but what about her other son? What about all the people who are dependent on her leadership as Lady of the keep? For that matter, if the Keep ceases to function, what will happen to Bran anyway? Catelyn's life is not simple and her duty is heavy to bear, the heavier with Ned having left for King's Landing to serve as the King's Hand, but in sitting by Bran for so long I think she is in service firstly to her emotions, not to Bran. This is what Robb alerts her to by challenging her as no-one else can, and in that he steps into manhood. No child could challenge his own mother like that.

I had a personal encounter with a substantial choice where duty and service were not clear a couple of years ago. It was not a matter of life and death, but for me and my family it was a big deal. My wife was pregnant with our son (now born, beautiful, very loved and called Samson), and I was not really happy in my job. I had been working slowly towards being able to go freelance for a while but it still felt like I was a little way off from being ready for that. I'd started to look at other possible jobs but that didn't feel right really. I chose to quit my job and set up on my own. To leave a secure job with a child on the way was by many people's standards pretty crazy and may have seemed a selfish act: I was, after all, following my dream. But it was actually thinking of my wife and son that made the decision clear for me. I didn't want to be a dad that comes home from work unhappy, frustrated, and bent out of shape. I didn't want to set that example for my son, or be that man for my wife. It is sometimes the case that if you want to be truly in service to your own sense of the greater good, then you have to do counter-intuitive things. I have to live with the consequences of my choice for good or ill. It still feels like it was the right choice for me, and for us as a family, but it has been tough along the way and I have needed to hang on to that sense of higher purpose – not just my own personal mission in life, but the higher purpose of being the best man, husband, and father that I can.

What I hope you can see from all this is that service and duty are complex and just as present in our lives as the lives of those in Westeros or the medieval world. Duty and service can be gifts if we can embrace them that way, but we must be mindful of the costs both to ourselves or others lest we become mindless servants, or fanatics of the cause. It is this caution which enables us to intelligently embrace a warrior's path of service to a higher purpose rather than enslaving ourselves and others to a dogmatic set of rules.

# Facing Death

# Chapter 6 – Facing Death

*Syrio: "Do you pray to the Gods?"*

*Arya: "The old and the new."*

*Syrio: "There is one God and his name is Death. And there is only
one thing we say to Death: "Not Today." "*[xliii]

Death is avoided in the modern world. That may
seem a strange thing to say, or an obvious thing to do but I
mean it more than just as a consequence. We mostly avoid
talking about it, facing it, planning for it, or indeed
embracing it when it comes. It is the one completely
inevitable event of our lives and yet we work so hard to
avoid it. Even though Syrio Forel in the scene I have
quoted above is speaking of denying death, he does so with
a familiarity. He does so with Death as his God, and a God
he is familiar enough with to say "No" to! While he will
keep saying "No" as long as he can, he has no fear of death
and he faces it bravely, even with a sense of humour. I like
this kind of relationship to death and in some ways it seems
psychologically healthier to me than avoidance. Just as life
is suffering (one of the core teachings of Buddhism I
touched on in Chapter 2), life is also going to end. I would
rather meet Death as a familiar friend than as an implacable
enemy. In terms of illness, we tend to try and fend off
death by any means and for as long as possible almost
regardless of the quality of life that can be had. I don't
think all medical professionals think this way (I've met

plenty who don't) but many do, and certainly I'd say the prevailing Western cultural view is that death should be avoided at all costs. I find this sad, and in many indigenous shamanic cultures there are and were practices of healing people into death. I'm not talking about euthanasia as the monstrous abuse of authority that it is so-often painted as in the press. I'm talking about compassion. Sometimes someone is just on their way out of this world and the most compassionate thing we can do is help them to leave us with as much as possible dignity, grace, and peace. Whether they go on to another life in another form is a matter of belief, but it is my faith that death is a transformation, not an ending. That's part of how I have made my peace with it.

As with Service in the last chapter, the matter of facing death resonates strongly with Samurai culture. It is considered by some, and George Leonard[17] spoke of this, that the reason why the Samurai were so feared in battle is because they faced it as if they were already dead – they had nothing to lose. This quote from the Hagakure illustrates the mindset well:

*"Meditation on inevitable death should be performed daily. Every day when one's body and mind are at peace, one should meditate upon being ripped apart by arrows, rifles, spears and swords, being carried away by surging waves, being thrown into the midst of a great fire, being struck by lightning, being shaken to death by a great earthquake, falling from thousand-foot cliffs, dying of disease or committing seppuku at the death of one's master. And every day*

---

17 Grandfather of the Human Potential Movement, author of numerous books including 'Mastery' and 'The Silent Pulse', respected Martial Artist and creator of the Samurai Game®

*without fail one should consider himself as dead.*

*There is a saying of the elders' that goes, "Step from under the eaves and you're a dead man. Leave the gate and the enemy is waiting." This is not a matter of being careful. It is to consider oneself as dead beforehand."*[xliv]

Although this has a much more serious tone than Syrio's "Not today" it has a similar feel to me. Syrio knows he is dead, just not today! He belongs to Death but he is not suicidal. Neither were the Samurai, though their philosophy could be mistaken for it. As I talked about in Chapter 1, it is a well known phenomenon that a nearness to death, brings out a desire to feel more alive. I believe that it is also the case that if we embrace the reality of death, we can more readily embrace the reality of our lives. By knowing death we can live more fully. In the Toltec tradition[18] this is sometimes referred to as 'Death as Advisor.' We bring death closer to our lives that this may inform our living and encourage us to live more fully, with greater presence, and a clearer sense of what is really important to us. To quote Casteneda:

*"Only the idea of death makes a warrior sufficiently detached so that he is capable of abandoning himself to anything. He knows his death is stalking him and won't give him time to cling to anything so he tries, without craving, all of everything."*

---

18 A shamanic tradition of Central America, best known in the writing of Carlos Casteneda although he is by no means the only exponent or writer on the subject, 2 others being Theun Mares, and Don Miguel Ruiz

The quality of non-attachment when embracing death in this way is also explored in the Hagakure:

*"If a warrior is not unattached to life and death, he will be of no use whatsoever. The saying that "all abilities come from one mind" sounds as though it has to do with sentient matters, but it is in fact a matter of being unattached to life and death. With such non-attachment one can accomplish any feat. Martial arts and the like are related to this insofar as they can lead to the Way[19]."[xlv]*

It is another commonly observed phenomenon that when people know that they are going to die soon, at some point a kind of peace and clarity may set in. They can accept it and they make very deliberate and clear choices about how they want to spend their last days. I'm not talking about blowing their savings on a spree, I'm talking more about appreciating life's simple pleasures and having their loved-one's about them. Where before choices seemed muddy and complex, now the right course seems very clear. King Robert Baratheon has some of this kind of clarity when he lies dying, having been gored by a boar while hunting. He asks Ned to stop Daenerys Targaryen's assassination if he can and acknowledges Ned's wisdom in opposing the killing in the first place. He realises that he hasn't spent time being any kind of father to Joffrey and asks Ned to teach Joff to be a better man that he (Robert) is. He can see very clearly the ways that he has not acted responsibly as a King. Imagine if you could live every-day

---

19 By 'Way' they mean the Way as in Tao, Dao or Do, which means
'The Way' and is your path through life and the greater flow of
life itself

with that kind of clarity, presence and peace. If you could see yourself and your life so clearly that your every decision becomes a simple one. I believe that, that is possible if we really embrace this aspect of the warrior's way. Death can be our advisor on how to live our lives more wisely.

In a way, the words of house Stark are a grimmer version of this kind of embracing of death. As Maester Aemon of the Night's Watch says:

*"The Stark's are always right in the end: Winter is coming. This one will be long and dark things will come with it."*

Like so many of us with death, the people of Westeros are often in denial about Winter. In many ways it is symbolic of the forces of death in their world. The inexorable march of winter and the dark creatures that come with the cold. The mass denial of the existence of the White Walkers is part of this. It has been a very long time since they were last seen, but it is one thing to think they may have been vanquished for good and quite another to dismiss them as fairy-tales, like Tyrion Lannister. I'm sure he is only representative of the majority of those who live in the South though.

I think facing death is vital for living a full life. At one point Renly Baratheon says:

*"My brother thinks anyone who hasn't been to war isn't a man."*[xlvi]

I don't agree with King Robert on that, but I might go so far as to say that anyone who hasn't faced death isn't a warrior. I don't mean you need to have faced a life-threatening situation (though arguably every day is that, if we did but know it!), I'm talking about dealing with the reality of death in our lives. In some ways that is almost easier when someone near to us has died. I know for myself that I faced death in a way I never had before when my mum died, for instance. But I don't know whether even that is necessary to find it in ourselves to really accept the reality of death. I feel confident that I was more prepared than I would have been otherwise for my mum's death by the fact I had faced death in a shamanic[20] burial ritual (where I was buried in the ground overnight in a ceremonial act while studying shamanic healing and initiation). The fact is that things are dying all the time. Any ending of anything is a little death. A moment emerges, happens and then is gone – it will never return in that form ever again. That is as conclusive as death gets. Just as I think we have learned to avoid the greater reality of death in the modern world, I think we do pretty well at avoiding facing the truth of these little deaths[21]. We either want to try and make something last forever, or we want to throw it away as soon as it looks like it's coming to an end so we can pretend it never happened. Either is an avoidant strategy. We need to learn to face our endings, to face the many deaths that occur in our lives and to find the gift in them, otherwise we are destined to repeatedly be battered

---

20 Shamanism is the study of indigenous, tribal healing, visionary, and initiatory practices
21 I have included an article from my blog in the appendices which says more about endings

by misery. Would you rather meet death as a familiar friend or an implacable enemy?

Another gift that embracing death can give us is bonding. When we face death together with others, we are connected by having shared the experience. This is well documented as a psychological phenomenon amongst soldiers, police officers, and firemen – when you have literally faced death together, there is a trust that transcends whether you like each other or not. There is a moment when Ned Stark and Ser Barristan Selmy subtly acknowledge this. They are walking together speaking about Ser Huw of the Vale, there is a clear sense of the respect they have for each other and they are speaking like old friends. Ser Barristan says:

*"Life is strange. Not so many years ago we fought as enemies at the Trident."*

I like this moment between two old warriors and it reminds me of something I have witnessed in The Samurai Game® which is a game of awareness which is often used to explore matters of leadership and choice. Within the game, the players are in 2 'Clans' doing battle, and one of the things which can happen is that the players can experience a metaphorical death. They are dead within the Game. It is part of what brings a sense of import and consequence to the Game itself, but it also means that part of the game can be experiencing a ritual death. What I have witnessed there and experienced myself when playing the Game is that even though it is a ritual death, people still come out profoundly connected with each other because they have gone through the experience together. I have heard many people speak of how affected they were when team-mates died in battle. Even people from opposite clans who were fighting during the Game, come out connected by the experience of having fought, lived and died through the same Game. This has a very similar feel to me as the conversation between Ned Stark and Ser Barristan Selmy. In a surprising number of ancient indigenous tribal cultures they would have regular ritual battles between tribes. Sometimes it was at a certain time of the year and sometimes it was to resolve disputes. Either way, the goal was rarely to kill each other, it was to best the other clan. People were hurt but rarely killed. The First Nation American tradition of 'Counting Coup' was part of this kind of practice whereby it was considered a greater achievement to touch an opponent with an open hand in combat than to beat them fighting with weapons. Obviously when there were less people and the warriors were also the hunter-gatherers tribes could have wiped each other out in open warfare very fast so there is a basic wisdom I these practices but I think there may have been more to it than that. I think perhaps there was a way that the bonding and mutual respect that is fostered when facing each other in combat was being used to help bond the young men from different tribal groups so as older men they could more wisely collaborate for the good of their tribes. This is pure speculation but based on what I have read on the psychology and experience of soldiers, and what I have witnessed in the Samurai Game®, I have my suspicions. There is a quote from the Hagakure which I think Syrio, Ned and Barristan would appreciate:

*"A certain person said, "In the saint's mausoleum there is a poem that goes:*

> *If in one's heart*
>
> *He follows the path of sincerity,*
>
> *Though he does not pray,*
>
> *Will not the gods protect him?*

*What is this path of sincerity?"*

*A man answered him by saying, "You seem to like poetry. I will answer you with a poem.*

> *As everything in the world is but a sham,*
>
> *Death is the only sincerity.*

*It is said that becoming as a dead man in one's daily living is the following of the path of sincerity."*

Death is so often seen as a curse, and in Westeros it is embodied as one of the 7 faces of the god: The Stranger. No-one wishes to look on it's face and it is feared more than worshipped. What I offer here is that Death can be our wisest advisor and can even be the presence which gives greatest clarity, meaning, and focus to our lives. Death is coming for all of us, so I'll ask you again:

**Do you wish to meet Death as a familiar friend, or as an implacable enemy?**

# Honour

# Chapter 7 – Honour

*"There are few men of honour in the capital. You are one of them. I would like to believe I am another, strange as that may seem."*

— *Varys*

So much in the collective psyche of Westeros seems to revolve around matters of honour, and yet, so much of what we witness in the lead characters involves dishonourable action and deceit. Throughout Westeros, Jaime Lannister is known as 'The Kingslayer' and to some degree is viewed and treated as an oathbreaker and therefore at some basic level untrustworthy. I can understand that, if you can't trust a person's word then it's hard to gauge what they will or won't do in any situation. That someone's actions match their words shows a basic quality of integrity and helps to engender a deep trust so without this, where do you stand with someone? In everyday life, I know for myself that if someone repeatedly says they'll do something and then doesn't deliver, I start to lode trust in them. Not necessarily in a big way but in that I will choose not to rely on them in the future. I start to have a working assumption that they might let me down. I have experienced this happening when I have let people down too and I understand it – I think it's a common way of operating whether it is conscious or unconscious. Jaime Lannister's case is interesting though because many, if not

114

most of the people that treat him as untrustworthy also recognise that the King he killed needed to die. He was, unjust, actually mad, and spiralling out of control. Because of his paranoia the Kingsguard were potentially the only people in a position to ill King Aerys too. Jaime and Ned Stark have a dialogue about it at one point in the story which includes this exchange:

Jaime:

*"500 men just stood there and watched. All the great knights of the seven kingdoms, you think anyone said a word? Lifted a finger? No Lord Stark. 500 men and this room was silent as a crypt. Except for the screams of course, and the mad King laughing. And later, when I watched the mad King die, I remembered him laughing as your father burned. It felt like justice."*

Ned:

*"Is that what you tell yourself at night? That you're a servant of justice? That you were avenging my father when you shoved a sword in Aerys Targaryen's back?"*

Jaime:

*"Tell me, if I'd stabbed the mad King in the belly instead of the back, would you admire me more?"*

Ned:

*"You served him well. When serving was safe."*[xlvii]

There is a kind of hypocrisy about how Jaime Lannister is treated. He did something that arguably needed doing, but because he broke an oath in doing so he is ostracised for it. There is a particularly sharp edge to this with Ned Stark because mad King Aerys murdered his father, brother and sister. You would have thought that if anyone would understand Jaime's actions, Ned would. There is definitely other kinds of water under the bridge between these two but much of the distrust seems to stem from this fact that Jaime broke his oath as a member of the Kingsguard and killed his King. The inherent dilemma in Jaime's position and the way he is judged exemplifies the two ends of the spectrum around honour for me: taking action because you believe it to be the right thing, and taking action because you believe it to be the necessary thing. These may not seem like opposites and I think they are not mutually exclusive – the best acts fulfil both criteria – but as motivations they are very different.

In many ways these two ends of the spectrum when looking at honour are perfectly embodied by the heads of the houses who are the biggest players in this first part of the story: Eddard Stark and Tywin Lannister. Ned Stark counts honour so highly that, as I have discussed earlier here, sometimes it blinds him and he may even fail in the task for the sake of trying to perform it honourably. Tywin seems to have eyes only for the prize and the ends can justify any means. It seems to me ironic that two men of such different outlooks could both have the honour of their houses so central in their minds, and yet they both do. My sense is that Ned is concerned with preserving the legacy of his family – he is past focused. His castle of Winterfell is ancient and it's very foundations are filled with a crypt holding statues of the  great Lords of Stark from the past. There is a sense of Ned being is service to his honour – as shows in the moment when he chooses to go and serve as Hand to the King and says to Catelyn "I have no choice".  Tywin is concerned with creating the legacy of his family as a seat of greatness for generations to come – he is future focused. This is very clearly expressed in a conversation he has with Jaime:

*"Your mother's dead. Before long I'll be dead. And you. And your brother, and your sister, and all her children. All of us dead, all of us rotting in the ground. It's the family name that lives on, it's all that lives on. Not your personal glory, not your honour, but family. Do you understand?"* [xlviii]

In some ways I think both Ned and Tywin concern themselves greatly with the honour of their Houses, but for Ned it is honour for the sake of doing what is right, for Tywin it is honour for the sake of the results it gets. Again we see his focus on ends rather than means. If these two great men are at either end of this spectrum then King Robert Baratheon sits in the middle – a pragmatist to Ned's idealist, but not the cold cynicism of Tywin. We see this in the scene where Robert has heard that Daenerys Targaryen is pregnant and want to have her killed:

Ned says:
*"You'll dishonour yourself forever if you do this!"*

Robert replies:

*"Honour? I've got seven kingdoms to rule. One King, seven kingdoms. Do you think honour keeps them in line? Do you think it's honour keeping the peace? It's fear, fear and blood!"*

I would prefer to think that a sense of honour is part of what keeps order in a society too but perhaps I am an idealist as well. Varys is an unlikely source of honour at first glance but as he says of himself in the quote at the start of this chapter, I think he is a man of honour. His is the honour that is worn very much on the inside. He doesn't care how people view him but he does try to do what he believes is the right thing for the realm. It is his own personal sense of honour he serves. While Ned is definitely most concerned with doing what he judges to be the honourable thing I'd say he is not unconcerned with how others see him. That is why he is so embarrassed and sensitive about his infidelity to Catelyn which led to Jon Snow's birth. Tyrion Lannister is another example of someone who definitely follows his own sense of honour, but doesn't care much what others think. His sense of honour comes out in how he treats people, like when he goes back to Winterfell on the way south from the Wall and has designed a special saddle to help Bran Stark. He also speaks very directly to Jon Snow about serving the honour of his house:

*"I must do my part for the honour of my house, wouldn't you agree? But how? Well, my brother has his sword, and I have my mind, and a mind needs books like a sword needs a whet-stone."*[xlix]

It is interesting that Tyrion later falls in with Bronn the sell-sword who's orientation around honour is so much like Tyrion's father Tywin. After Bronn uses numerous tricks, evasions and trips to beat Ser Vardis when Bronn stands as Tyrion's champion in a trial by combat Lysa Arryn (nee Tully) says:

*"You don't fight with honour."*

To which Bronn replies:

*"He did."* (indicating the man he has just killed)[1]

I could almost hear Tywin Lannister giving the same response, although I doubt he would have the same sense of humour or insolence that Bronn brings to the phrase.

Jaime Lannister holds the honour of his house very differently than Tyrion and is much more concerned with what people think of him. His father Tywin criticizes him for it saying:

*"You spend far too much time worrying what people think of you."*

To which Jaime replies:
*"I could care less what anyone thinks of me"*

Tywin responds:
*"Yeh well that's what you want other people to think of you."*

Tywin has nailed Jaime on this one – and no wonder he's his father! This part of the scene follows on from a conversation where Tywin asks why Ned Stark isn't dead. Jaime explains that one of their spearmen interfered when Jaime and Ned were in single combat. Jaime says:

*"It wouldn't have been clean."*[xii]

Not "It wouldn't have been right" or "Just", or "Fair." It is about how the win would have been perceived, and Jaime wanted to beat Ned Stark fair and square for the sake of his reputation. It was a matter of vanity for Jaime. For Tywin honour is a tool for getting a job done as we see very clearly later in this scene. When he speaks of why they must take Tyrion back (who has been arrested by Catelyn Stark):

*"He's a Lannister. He might be the lowest of the Lannisters but he's one of us. And every day that he remains a prisoner, the less our name commands respect."*

The honour of their house is a tool for wielding power and control for Tywin. Catelyn (supported by Ned) arrests Tyrion for the sake of seeing justice done, Tywin wants him back for the sake of preserving his power-base. The difference between the two Houses could not be more clearly symbolised than by this situation.

I'd say Jaime Lannister's relationship to honour is the most common in the overall story of 'Game of Thrones' although Tywin's perspective is born by a fair few as well. For Prince Joffery honour is all about people seeing him as a great King to be. It is driven by vanity, that is why he has to control and shame Sansa Stark so much: she witnessed Joffrey be shamed by Arya and her wolf. His fragile ego can't stand for this to be the case so Sansa must be shamed continually so that Joffrey can keep his own shame at bay. The Knight of Flowers, Ser Loras Tyrell, seems a fine example of knighthood indeed but again it is all about his vanity. He uses a trick with his horse being in heat (wanting to mate) to beat Ser Gregor Clegane in the tourney. If his sense of honour was as internally driven as Ned Stark then he would never use such a trick – though I grant you he might die as a result of it judging by Gregor's track record.

One of the shadows and dangers of having a strong sense of the honour of your House (or family) is the potential for a sense of entitlement. Viserys Targaryen embodies this more clearly than anyone else – he is almost a caricature of this trait at times. When he is selling Daenerys into her marriage with Khal Drogo he says:

*"When they write the history of my reign, sweet sister, they will say it began today."*[xii]

Talk about counting your chickens before they have hatched! His sense of entitlement rears it's ugly head again and again often at a cost to Daenerys until eventually it proves Viserys' downfall when he threatens Daenerys' life, her child and draws a sword in the sacred city of Vaes Dothrak where no sword should even be carried, let alone drawn. He is given the crown he feels the world owes him as a bowl of molten gold over the head and dies screaming.

Petyr Baelish – Lord Littlefinger – has a total disregard for any sense of honour. One of the places this shows up is when he is speaking to Ned Stark who he has agreed to help for the sake of his love of Catelyn (with whom he grew up). Ned says:

*"Lord Baelish, perhaps I was wrong to distrust you."*

To which Petyr replies:

*"Distrusting me was the wisest thing you've done since you climbed off your horse."*

Littlefinger places no value on his honour or that of anyone else and is happy to admit it openly. Part of what I see regarding honour which is shown clearly through the example of the characters is that honour is a lens through which we see the world. It colours our choices internally and it colours the way we judge the world 'out there'. Ned values honour highly for it's own sake and is generally very trustworthy so he expects the same of other people. Littlefinger doesn't care about honour and isn't very trustworthy so he, equally expects the same of others. They are both likely to be surprised at least some of the time!

What I take from all this and what I offer to you is that your honour is entirely personal to you. It will of course be very connected with your honour code, whatever form that takes and whether that is a conscious thing you have set down or an unconscious or even unconsidered set of assumptions, beliefs and values. Your honour is what you make of it. Peter Hobart puts it beautifully:

*"One's honour is worth exactly as much as it's owner decides it is. For some, it is an inconvenient, unwieldy notion. Since it serves no concrete purpose, they give it little thought. For the practitioner of*

*Kishido[22], it is one of the few possessions of any consequence. Like one's word, its present measure is defined by past performance. For those descended from an honourable line, it is a sacred inheritance to be safeguarded at all costs. For every one, it will be a legacy – either good or bad. It is merely borrowed for a season.'[xliii]*

---

22 Kishido is the Japanese word for the 'Way of the Western Knight' (just like Bushido is the Way of the Samurai). It is used in Hobart's book as an acknowledgement of a mixed tradition where Westerners are training in a traditional Eastern art.

# Humility

# Chapter 8 – Humility

*"Humility does not mean thinking less of yourself than of other people, nor does it mean having a low opinion of your own gifts. It means freedom from thinking about yourself at all."*

*~William Temple*

Humility is often thought of as being in some way small or unnoticeable but that is not the true meaning of humility. Another misinterpretation is denying or your own abilities – being good at something but pretending you're not. This is false modesty and has nothing to do with true humility, indeed, in my experience of when I have done this myself and in when I have seen others do it, the person usually has a high opinion of their own abilities but wants others to think them modest. I know when I was younger I was very prone to this kind of false modesty (and it is generally more typical in the UK than, say, the US). If you'd asked me at the time I would have sworn blind that I believed that I was 'OK' at something I was excellent at, but I can say with confidence now that on reflection this concealed a kind of arrogance. On some level I so strongly believed in my own entitlement to admiration that I would 'play small' knowing that people would complement me anyway – and if they didn't would feel hurt they hadn't noticed! It's a minor form of craziness but I don't think I will have been alone in this pattern. It's not entirely comfortable to admit to even now but I've worked on it a fair bit and got better at holding it with more integrity.

Certainly some of what sponsored this behaviour was an insecurity about being seen as arrogant but that was not least of all because deep down I was arrogant! There is a beautiful example of this from Jaime Lannister in a conversation with Ned Stark. As we saw in a scene I have previously quoted, Tywin says that Jaime is very concerned with how people perceive him and we see the truth of that here. Jaime is without question incredibly gifted as a swordsman, but he is arrogant about it too – but doesn't want to be seen as arrogant as well as an oath-breaker. In this scene Ned has just made a pointed comment about how Jaime's armour doesn't have a scratch on it, to which Jaime replies:

*"People have been swinging at me for years but they always seem to miss."*

and Ned says:

*"You've chosen your opponents wisely then."*[xiv]

Jaime's comment tries to imply his own great skill while passing it off as other people's errors. Ned's response is, to my mind, perfect in the way he hands Jaime back both his own skill in the matter and an implication that his skill may not lie where he believes: not in honourable swordsmanship but political conniving. While Ned shows he lacks political astuteness and cunning in the rest of his time at King's Landing, in this exchange he plays it very well.

True humility doesn't try to hide anything, it is just realistic and honest. In this way it is very linked to self knowledge. In order to be truly humble you have to know exactly how good you are, and how much you have yet to learn. That's humility. It's not about pretending to be small or unskilled, or without value, it is about knowing exactly where you stand, owning that place, and regardless of how good you are or not, still being open to learning. I have come across rank beginners in numerous fields who still manage to take an arrogant stance and close themselves to learning. Equally I have come across world-class professionals who are still willing to listen to total beginners and derive real learning from those conversations. In my judgement, that's humility.

Some years ago I read an interesting interview with a Christian Minister who was talking about meekness[lv] in the context of Christ saying "The meek shall inherit the Earth." Again, a lot of people interpret this as meaning that people who waft about pretending that they're 'really not very important' are actually going to end up being the most important people (another example of repressed arrogance and entitlement if ever I saw one...). What this Minister was saying, was that the original meaning of the word 'meek' was totally different than this. He said that 'meek' originally was like a really well trained stallion: incredibly powerful, but that power being contained, controlled, channelled and harnessed to a purpose. Reading that I could see how the meek would inherit the Earth! Indeed, who else would? This feels very like the misunderstanding around humility. I see a humble person as someone who is absolutely aware of their own power, but who wields it wisely and is just as aware of their own vulnerability too. As Charles Haddon Spurgeon said:

*"Humility is to make a right estimate of one's self."*

It is about being the best of yourself with self-awareness but without self-consciousness. This is a subtle distinction which became much clearer to me at Drama School. I thought I was being self-aware as I was on stage but from the feedback I was getting it became clear that I was actually self-conscious in a way that was not helpful. It was like I was constantly observing myself and this kept me from being really present and responsive to what I was involved in. Self-awareness is something else entirely. It is a kind of expanded awareness which allows you to interact with your environment more consciously without taking you out of contact with the moment that is happening. It's a tough shift to make especially if, as was the case for me, the bit of you that is observing what you're doing is also criticising it. What I'm describing here is often talked about as the difference between 'doing' and 'being'. There is an old saying that:

*"A weak person pretends to be strong, a strong person just is."*

Part of what's intended here is not "...a strong person just is strong" but that "...a strong person just is." They "just are." Again, it is about 'being' something rather than 'doing' something. If you 'are' it, you don't have to 'do' it. Syrio makes a similar point when he is first teaching Arya Stark:

*"Boy, Girl. You are a sword. That is all."*[xlvi]

Syrio is emphasising just 'being' rather than becoming overly self-conscious about how you see yourself too. There is a state of internal congruence which comes with this kind of 'being' state, a foundation of integrity and authenticity. It was this authenticity which was missing when I was first studying at Drama School and which I had to work towards, and it is this authenticity which to me is a very clear sign of humility. For me, when someone is truly humble, they are authentic. They are at peace with who they are and they live and breathe it comfortably in every moment. Obviously everyone has tough moments or slips up, but that's OK too when you really find humility – after all, you've got nothing to prove. As G.K. Chesterton said:

*"It is always the secure who are humble."*

Jon snow who has always had so much to prove as a bastard is in some ways freed of his self-consciousness when he gets to the Wall and this helps him to grow into the kind of man people will follow and enables him to become a leader amongst the new recruits he trains with. As His Uncle Benjen tells him when he reaches the Wall:

*"Here a man gets what he earns, when he earns it."*[xvii]

No matter how much poorer his birth was than the true-born heirs he grew up with, Jon was born to a noble father and doesn't even realise he is 'putting on airs and graces'. Benjen brings him up short and living the reality of becoming a man of the Night's Watch makes Jon grow up fast. The moment Jon gets assigned to being a Steward instead of the Ranger he has always dreamed of being is another defining moment for him, when Sam helps him see the value of his new role serving Lord Commander Mormont, but none-the-less it is another layer of Jon's pride stripped away. I'd say he is a better man for it, and in that moment takes another step towards true humility.

There is a quote from the Hagakure which has a similar resonance to what Syrio says to Arya and speaks to me of a state of 'being' which is very connected to humility:

*"Among other things, the Way of the Samurai requires that he realise that something may occur at any moment to test the depth of his resolution, and day and night he must sort out his thoughts and prepare a line of action. Depending on the circumstances, he may win or lose. But avoiding dishonour is quite a separate consideration from winning or losing.... The veteran Samurai thinks not of victory or defeat but merely fights insanely to the death."*[xviii]

In this the Samurai is totally in service to their mission, totally present in every moment because they have no room in their thoughts for winning or losing. They set aside any concerns or anxiety about the outcome and dedicate themselves completely to the task. There is no self-consciousness here, what others think of you is unimportant – there is no thought of self at all – it is all about whole-hearted dedication. There is a fierce kind of authenticity which blossoms naturally from this quality of commitment, there is a necessity to be incredibly aware so that whatever happens the Samurai can face it. For me this quote links humility with responsibility and honour. The samurai in this example is not trying to be something, he's just being (humility) there is no space in his mindset for anything else. He strives for success but is not attached to it because he knows that he cannot control the circumstances and may win or lose (responsibility), he can only marshal his resolve and prepare a line of action. He commits himself completely knowing that honour is not about winning or losing but acquitting yourself with courage, integrity, and dedication. In this vision of honour, it is purely about your commitment to that which you serve – your higher purpose. There is a moment when Cersei sees something akin to this in Ned Stark and while she is scornful about what she sees, I admire it:

Cersei (speaking about Robert):
*"...You'll try your best to pick up the pieces"*

Ned:
*"If that's my job then so be it."*

Cersei:
*"You're just a soldier aren't you? You take your orders and you carry on. I suppose it makes sense, your older brother was trained to lead and you were trained to follow."*

Ned:
*"I was also trained to kill my enemies your Grace."*

Cersei:
*"As was I."*[lix]

Sadly, we know where this conflict ends for Ned, but in this moment as I say I can admire him. He knows that being King Robert's Hand will be tough but he is prepared to face that, and there is no thought of glory, power, or the admiration from others in Ned's acceptance of the task. He does it because he believes it is the right thing to do. I might question his wisdom about this decision to some extent but in the terms of the quote from the Hagakure, I cannot question his resolve. Win or lose, Ned will keep fighting.

I think humility is a vital quality for a warrior to develop because it enables a state whereby you can let go of your own ego enough to be present, open, aware, and constantly learning. Fortunately the martial environment also serves as a fantastic training ground for humility. As Daniele Bolelli discusses in his excellent book 'On the Warrior's Path':

*"Competing in combat sports teaches that no matter how good you become, there will always be someone better than you, or luckier than you. No matter how much you prepare, you come to realise that everyone loses. Everyone dies. Everyone gets caught in the end. This is the most important thing that combat sports can teach us. They take all illusions of invincibility away and teach us how to deal with defeat. Even if by some miracle, you end up being the most fearless, amazing fighter who ever lived, and no one can ever defeat you, your enemies outside of the ring – old age, sickness, and death – will catch up with you. Everyone gets caught in the end. No exceptions made."*[x]

This is why humility goes together with being on the warriors path: it's hard to be arrogant when you really face death, or at least defeat, on a regular basis. In some ways, even just the learning process in martial arts is one of constant defeat. I remember training in Tai Chi, and I would just be getting the hang of something, just starting to feel like I'd 'got it' (whatever 'it' was) and as my teacher saw this he'd say "Ah, I think you're ready for the next stage." With this next level of learning I'd go back to feeling like a clumsy beginner again. It was hard to maintain any arrogance in the face of this! I had a similar experience, and one which perhaps correlates more clearly with the world of Westeros when I used to train in medieval European weapons and take part in re-enactment displays. I got to a stage where I had a reasonable level of skill and could hold my own in fighting most of the other guys. I felt good about that. But as with the Tai Chi, the path wouldn't allow me to keep hold of that for long. Fighting in front of a crowd of a couple of hundred people is a whole other experience than on the training ground. My awareness would be much harder to hold in sharp focus on my opponent and when the adrenalin is flowing the world changes. Even more stark was the difference between fighting one-on-one and fighting in a melee involving multiple opponents. It's messy, noisy, confusing, and just plain hard to do well. No matter how good I thought I'd got, the challenge of the martial environment will always knock you off your pedestal eventually. As Bolelli says, if the other guy is luckier than you, or even just when ageing or illness starts to catch up with you, sooner or later if you lack humility, you will be humbled. My experience in re-enactment fighting showed me how vulnerable I was, how far from expert I was, and at a basic level how easily I could get myself killed in a real combat. These may seem like fairly negative things to learn about myself, but I see them as profoundly valuable learning and while it can be tough to find out you're not as good as you thought you were, it's important. I didn't discover I was bad at fighting with a sword, I just found out more precisely how good I was, and how much I had yet to learn. I knew much more clearly where I stood on my path after the first time I fought in a melee.

We seem as a culture in the modern Western world to have developed a strong addiction to invulnerability. We all want to be flawless experts right now. There seems to be very little value given to the Elder, the old-hand or the veteran. If we can have a wunderkind, a prodigy, an early high-flyer, or young genius then that's what we want: someone who has never made a mistake, and who, armoured with their own arrogance, we can believe (contrary to all historical evidence) will never make a mistake. I think humility has a core of vulnerability and rare is the person who is truly humble without having made a mistake. Jack Cirie – a combat veteran and ex-senior officer in the US Marines, quoted by Richard Strozzi Heckler, said:

*"Believing you can be perfect is the fatal imperfection. Believing you are invulnerable is the ultimate vulnerability. Being a warrior doesn't mean winning or even succeeding. It means risking and failing and risking again, as long as you live."*[lxi]

It both takes and teaches humility to be willing to fail, and any real risk may end in failure. It only takes misfortune for anything to end in failure so for me, humility is an invaluable capacity in any endeavour. Again in this quote we see the connection with responsibility too in terms of letting go of success or 'winning' as the vital outcome of your work. None of this is an excuse for mediocrity, this is not self-sabotage or empty failure. It is an acknowledgement that the odds are we are all going to face failure of one kind or another in our lives. If we are to make best use of those moments then we have to be ready to embrace our vulnerability, have the humility to realise when we have failed, to admit it, and then perhaps most important of all, to learn from what has taken place so when we step into taking the next of life's many risks we are better equipped. In this way, humility is what gives birth to wisdom. That is why wisdom is mostly the province of older folk. I have seen in my work with young people – especially high-flyers – that there is a sense of invincibility in the young. They haven't experienced such deep senses of grief and failure yet, they still think that they might be the one exception to the rule that's bullet-proof. There is a perfect example of this in the very first scene of the 'Game of Thrones' series when a young lord is leading a Ranging party north of the Wall. He is accompanied by two experienced Rangers who, once they have seen that the Wildlings they were tracking are dead, say they should all turn back to the Wall. He ignores them and even mocks them, insisting that they all carry on and examine the Wildling camp further. This is even against Lord Commander Mormont's commands, and as it turns out, arguably it is the young lord's arrogance that gets him and one of the other men killed by the Others. Perhaps if they'd turned back when the two Rangers wanted to, they'd all have lived to tell the tale. He thinks he knows better, and it gets him killed.

Over the years, if nothing else does it, for many of us parenthood will change this sense of invulnerability. I have never felt so helpless as in some of the times I have shared with my son when he is really distressed and I can't do anything to make it OK for him. I just have to be with him in his upset, swallow my need to 'fix it' and embrace rediscovering my humility. My son might see me as all powerful in his little world but I'm in trouble if I buy into that. There are some things I can't do anything about no matter how much I might want to. There is a deep and undervalued wisdom to be gained from parenthood itself, but it is a painful learning-ground at times. I think it takes a warrior to be a great parent. As I have quoted from Ned Stark before:

*"War was easier than daughters."*[lxii]

His brother Benjen Stark shows both his wisdom and his humility when he says to Tyrion Lannister:

*"It's not the wildlings giving me sleepless nights. You've never been north of the Wall, so don't tell me what's out there."*

He's not saying there are White Walkers or other kinds of monsters but he has seen enough strangeness in the world to have the humility to admit there might be. He is by no means playing small – he's challenging Tyrion Lannister on his arrogance, but neither is he trying to lord his own expertise over Tyrion either. Benjen might be one of the most experienced Rangers on the Wall, but he is wise enough to know how much he doesn't know. Being able to embrace both these things is humility and wisdom both. As Rick Warren says of humility:

*"Humility is not thinking less of yourself, it's thinking of yourself less."*

And as David Brooks describes wisdom:

*"Wisdom doesn't consist of knowing specific facts or possessing knowledge of a field. It consists of knowing how to treat knowledge: being confident but not too confident; adventurous but grounded. It is a willingness to confront counterevidence and to have a feel for the vast spaces beyond what's known."*[xiii]

For a concise but poetic definition of humility I might draw on what David Brooks says to put it like this:

Humility is about being adventurous but grounded, and having a feel for the vast spaces beyond what is known.

# Mercy

# Chapter 9 – Mercy

*"My father understands mercy when there is room for it."*

*- Robb Stark*

Mercy itself is not a commonly talked about subject in the modern world. I think this is because in order to be merciful with someone, you have to have power over them, and certainly in the modern Western world, we don't commonly think like that. There are many places where one person has power over another, but we like the ideas of democracy and equality more than the true practice of these things so it is more comfortable not to speak of 'power over' directly. As such, mercy is largely left out of the dialogue too. For me, mercy is very connected to many other ideas and ideals though, such as: respect, reserve, generosity, benevolence, compassion, and forgiveness. I offer these as an initial broadening of the dialogue in the hope that it helps you to set this idea in a wider context, and one which feels more relevant to modern life.

There are so many examples of people acting with a lack of mercy that I don't really want to get into it. The world of Westeros in this time of war, and particularly the world of Lord's and Lady's at court is riddled with selfish, arrogant, dishonest, and abusive behaviour. Cersei, Joffery, Tywin Lannister, and Ser Gregor Clegane might top the list for vicious, unmerciful monsters in their own unique ways, (even Jaime and the Hound have softer moments) but there is so much of it, to detail it would be depressing. So, as I spoke of at the beginning of this book, in this chapter perhaps even more than others I am going to focus on the moments where people shine rather than when they cast shadows.

Robb Stark, who's quote I have begun the chapter with is one of the clearest examples of how mercy can be wielded wisely, and powerfully. It is a sad irony that his father, from whom he clearly learned this wisdom, is at least partially undone by his merciful heart. In fact, several of Ned Stark's children seem to have learned mercy from their father, with varying outcomes. I will discuss Ned and Robb and some other examples, but let's begin with Robb as he is the shining light in this trait.

Robb's gift for wise mercy surfaces once Ned and Catelyn have both gone south and Robb is left to be Lord of Winterfell. When Tyrion Lannister visits on his way back from the Wall, Robb gives him a frosty welcome at first because he distrusts the Lannisters – and for good reason. However, when Tyrion offers the designs for a saddle which may enable Bran to ride again saying:

*I have a tender spot in my heart for cripples, bastards and broken things.* "[lxiv]

Robb softens and offers for Tyrion to stay at Winterfell. Tyrion's act is a merciful one itself, and Robb responds in kind, wisely to my mind as I am not convinced Tyrion was involved in Bran's 'accident'. This is hinted at in some of his conversations with Lady Catelyn after she arrests him.

The next time we see Robb's merciful side come out is when the group of wildlings try and kidnap Bran when he is riding in the woods. Only one of them is left alive (Osha) and he allows her to live and be a servant in Winterfell. This could seem like a foolish move to welcome an enemy into your home – even in chains – but she turns out to be trustworthy and much of what we see from Robb in his decision-making suggests to me both a deep, thoughtful intelligence, and a high degree of intuition.

The next two examples of Robb's wise mercy occur once he has called the banners to go to war and I would say that they are both instrumental in his success as a commander. First is when he is feasting the lords of the North who have come with their men to answer Robbs call as their liege lord. Jon Umber, know as the Greatjon, and one of the most experienced and fierce warriors amongst the lords gathered is saying that he should lead Robb's vanguard, and that he will not follow the Glover's whom Robb has given that task. Robb says that if the Greatjon won't do as he's told then he can go home and Robb will come back after the war and hang him as an oath-breaker. The Greatjon is furious and draws a blade, in response to which, Robb's direwolf leaps across the table and knocks him over, proceeding to bite off two of his fingers! Robb could have the Greatjon killed on the spot but again his wise mercy emerges and he offers the Greatjon an honourable way out:

Robb:
*"My lord-father taught me it was death to bare steel against your liege-lord. Doubtless the Greatjon only meant to cut my meat for me."*

There is a pregnant pause as everyone holds their breath to see what will happen...

The Greatjon:
*"Your meat....(he still sounds angry and everyone remains uncertain)... Is bloody tough!"*

Jon and Robb begin to laugh and soon everyone joins in.[lxv]

This is a defining moment for Robb because if he does what the Greatjon wants him to do then all these older lords will see him as a boy and he will lose the command in that instant. Equally if he is too harsh he could sow dissent amongst the very men he most needs behind him, before they have even begun their march to war. He manages to strike a perfect balance and in his merciful treatment of Jon Umber, wins respect from all of them and a staunch support from Jon.

The second of these examples of Robb's wise mercy is when he and his lords are planning their first direct move against the two Lannister armies, one led by Tywin, one by Jaime. As they are speaking some of Robb's men march in a Lannister scout whom they have captured. Robb asks him questions about what he's seen and how many men he's counted. It is clear everyone believes he should be killed and Ser Rodrick (who was the master of arms at Winterfell) says:

*"You don't have to do this yourself, your father would understand.."*

Robb cuts him off:
*"My father understands mercy when there is room for it. And he understands honour. And courage. Let him go."*

Lady Catelyn interrupts:
*"Robb."*

Robb moves closer to the scout and says:
*"Tell Lord Tywin winter is coming for him.   20,000 northerners marching south to see if he really does shit gold."*

The scout:
*"Yes my Lord, thank you my Lord."*

And for me there is a real sense of respect and gratitude from the scout.[lxvi]

This could seem like foolishness, and certainly Jon Umber challenges his authority again, but Robb is not only doing what he believes is right in treating even his enemies with dignity and honour, but he is sowing the seed of his plan.  He has fed Tywin Lannister false information which is what enables Robb to divert Tywin and go and attack Jaime's smaller force and catch them by surprise.  In both of these examples I'm sure you can see how Robb manages to be both merciful and powerful.  He stays focused on his true enemy – Tywin Lannister – and gives mercy as a gift which is part of what wins people to his cause and makes him a great leader.  Mercy is not about being soft, or fluffy, or a push-over.  Mercy is about wielding your power wisely and compassionately and Robb demonstrates that masterfully in these moments.

Exercising mercy does not always end well though as we see in for Ned Stark.  When Ned has been imprisoned, Varys visits and asks him:

*"What madness led you to tell the Queen you'd learned the truth about Joffrey's birth?"*

Ned replies:
*"The madness of mercy, that she might save her children."*

And later in the scene Varys says:

*"It wasn't the wine that killed Robert, nor the boar.... The wine slowed him down and the boar ripped him open, but it was your mercy that killed the King."*

While Varys can be wise in his observations about many things, and Ned is definitely acting out of mercy when he speaks to Queen Cersei, I would still contend that it was Ned's blind assumptions around matters of honour which killed the King, not his mercy. Ned's mercy led him to want to protect Cersei's children, his honour-blindness led Ned to judge Cersei and others by his own high standards and it is this misjudgement which killed the King in the way Varys is talking about. Honour is Ned's madness, not mercy. Ned seeks to be merciful in the matter of killing Daenerys Targaryen as well and it is this which first causes a rift between him and King Robert. Again, I would say that it is not Ned's mercy which gets him into trouble but his rigid ideas about honour. When he challenges Robert on his choice to murder the girl princess he says:

*"You will dishonour yourself forever if you do this."*

145

He appeals to Robert's honour, when Robert is a man of pragmatism so it is easy for him to dismiss Ned's perspective and tell the rest of his council:

*"Speak sense to this honourable fool."*[lxvii]

King Robert realises and admits on his death-bed that it was the wrong thing to do and Ned was the only one to challenge him. Perhaps if Ned had appealed to Robert differently he may have come to this realisation earlier and Ned's fate could have been a better one.

As I mentioned we see Ned's gift of mercy in some of his other children as well as Robb. Sansa has much more of his idealistic, trusting blindness, but we have glimpses of it in moments with Arya. However, Jon is the other of Ned's children who really seems to have learned to be merciful. We see this in various aspects of his character and behaviour, but it is most clear in his treatment of Samwell Tarly. Although at first he is tough with Sam and tries to tell him to 'toughen up' he swiftly realises that Sam just isn't built that way – and that doesn't mean he is not a worthwhile human being. I see it as one of Jon's defining moments, and one of the acts that most clearly sets him out as a leader amongst his batch of recruits for the Wall when he persuades them all to look after Sam:

*"Sam's no different than the rest of us. There's no place for him in the world so he's come here. We're not gonna' hurt him in the training yard any more, never again, no matter what Thorne says. He's our brother now and we're going to protect him."*[lxviii]

Jon shows here a great deal of maturity and compassion. This is really what mercy is about, and this is what power is about. He lives the Knight's oath to protect those weak and defenceless. In this environment Sam is pretty defenceless, and Jon is in a position of power due to his skill at arms. While democracy and equality are in so many ways wonderful things to strive for, one of the tragedies of the modern drive for these ideals is that we are forgetting the art of the responsible use of power. Everyone is so busy pretending that they don't have power, that they're just the same as you and me and we're all OK, that when people do have power, often they are not particularly conscious about how they wield it. Because people do become powerful. Power is really just about being influential so whether you have a formal position of leadership or not, you can be hugely influential if people choose to follow you, and by that influence you are powerful. At the US military academy at Westpoint, my friend Lance Giroux[23] told me they used to define a leader as:

*"Anyone who influences others to effective action."*

They may well still be using that definition. When talking about this, one of the examples Lance uses is: When a baby cries and it's mother picks it up, who's the leader?... It's the baby! The baby has influenced it's mother to take effective action. We are quite literally leading from birth, we are powerful through influence from birth. Anyone who has ever held and melted in the presence of a new-

---

23 Lance trained at Westpoint, served in the US army, and is now the Director of Allied Ronin Leadership Consultancy

born will attest to that. And yet unless you have a management job, most of us never receive any leadership training. It's not part of our schooling system in spite of it being such a core human capacity. Leadership, influence is about wielding our power wisely whether that power is big or small. Even if it's just with our friends or kids, we all have power. As I have said, I see mercy as being about wielding power wisely, responsibly, and compassionately. In this, while he may be flawed (as all of us are) Ned Stark is a wonderful example of leadership, and his sons Robb and Jon Snow have evidently learned something from him. I think if we can all learn to wield the power we have more wisely, responsibly and compassionately, then our world will be a better place. In walking the Warrior path we must embrace our own capacity for influence and power, and in this task, mercy is a better name for our sword than anything more glamorous, adventurous or overtly war-like. As my colleague Cathy Glass is fond of saying:

*"Kind eyes, sharp sword."*

We must find our clarity, courage, and fierceness to face life with authenticity and power. But we must do so always with loving intent.

I was recently reading Sam Sheridan's excellent book on martial arts and fighting 'A Fighter's Heart.' Towards the end there was a particularly intriguing section which spoke to me about the connection between the Warrior's path and love. In this, Sheridan is himself referencing a book ('On Aggression' by Konrad Lorenz). He says:

*"Lorenz studied tropical reef fish and geese, and used the observed behaviours to draw inferences about all vertebrates and thus ourselves. He first noticed that on the reef, "fish are far more aggressive towards their own species than any other" (outside of eating and being eaten, of course). The male fish viciously attack other male fish of the same species, the females the females, while allowing the myriad others to coexist peacefully.... He talks about geese and says that two furiously aggressive animals must bond and live together in a small space, all without weakening intra-species aggression. They have evolved inhibitors, behaviour-changing devices, that turns the aggression they normally feel towards others of their species into something else when they mate. The same thing, albeit in a more complex way, takes place among men and women of the same tribe or family unit... friendship is only found in animals with "highly developed intra-specific aggression"... the more aggressive the animal, the deeper the friendship. The ability to love and form bonds has evolved as a way to temper aggression, to turn it into something more powerful when defending hearth and home. Friendship and love are essentially evolutionary by-products of aggression.... That's the secret: It's all about love."*[lxix]

This may seem a little odd, even counter-intuitive, but it gives me hope and is further confirmation of something I have long suspected: If we can embrace the fierce warrior which resides in all our hearts', then that same warrior can teach us how to live together better, more peacefully, and with a greater capacity for love.

# Honesty

# Chapter 10 – Honesty

*"A lie will easily get you out of a scrape, and yet, strangely and beautifully, rapture possesses you when you have taken the scrape and left out the lie."*

~*Charles Edward Montague*[xx]

I am not going to draw out lots of examples and quotes here. The story of 'Game of Thrones is so riddled with despicable dishonesty and inspiring truths that you can see it very well for yourself. In some ways it is precisely these lies and truths which have formed the topic of every chapter thus far, they have been the illustrations for our brief wander down the Warrior's path.

What I want to bring to your attention here in this last chapter is that all of the other values, qualities, and principles I have spoken of are nothing without honesty. I have said before that all of these qualities are interdependent, that if one is undermined then the others are likely to fall, but really without honesty it all falls apart. That is why this is called a 'Path' or a 'Way', because while I can talk about parts of it, specific skills or capacities if you will, the truth of it is a whole way of being, not a set of reducible skills. These chapters with their themes point the way (or Way) towards a whole-hearted commitment to living life as a Warrior, not just having a hobby and doing some warrior stuff. So when I say that without honesty it all falls apart I'm not just talking about honesty with others, although that's an important, I am talking about honesty with yourself. In the privacy of your own mind, can you tell yourself the truth? It is so easy to embellish and invent a slightly better, slightly more attractive version of what happens in our lives. It is so seductive to re-tell our own stories in our minds in such a way that we come out slightly better, braver, more virtuous, or more generous of spirit than we were, but you can never improve what you can't see, and these little internal deceits camouflage our areas of greatest learning. You have to keep asking yourself the question:

"Am I being the person I have always dreamed of being?"

And answering as honestly as possible. Not so you can give yourself a hard time about it, but so you know where you stand. From that place you can face the truth and make choices. That is the best that anyone can do, and it is what will give you the power to shape your life as much as is humanly possible. It's a hard path to be this rigorously, or even ruthlessly honest with yourself, but as Montague's quote at the start of this chapter suggests, I think it's worth it.

As I spoke about in my introduction, I believe that part of what an epic story like 'Game of Thrones' offers us is inspiration. We can live through and learn with these great characters, and from that become better equipped to be the heroes of our own lives. What could be more important than that?

One of my favourite quotes speaks of the power of this eloquently, so I shall finish with that:

*"Don't ask yourself what the world needs; ask yourself what makes you come alive. And then go and do that. Because what the world needs is people who have come alive."*

*- Howard Thurman*

# Appendices

# Book List 1

## For living a learning about the Warrior's Path:

- A little book on finding your Way: Zen and the Art of Doing stuff - by Francis Briers
  - This is a book to help you take any activity and turn it into a 'Way' or life practice

- I have several more books out soon, listed in the front of this book, particularly 'My Tao Te Ching' if you are interested in Taoism and 'Paths' or 'Ways'; and 'The Art of Dad-Fu' if you're a father.

- Hagakure – The Way of the Samurai by Yamamoto Tsunetomo, translated by William Scott Wilson

- In Search of the Warrior Spirit – Teaching Awareness Disciplines to the Green Beret's by Richard Strozzi-Heckler

- On the Warrior's Path – Philosophy, Fighting and Martial Arts Mythology Daniele Bolelli

- Kishido – The Way of the Western Warrior by Peter Hobart

- A Fighter's Heart – by Sam Sheridan

- The Way of the Peaceful Warrior
  by Dan Millman

- Shambhala: The Sacred Path of the Warrior - by
  Chogyam Trungpa

- The Way of Aikido - by George Leonard

- Mastery - by George Leonard

- The Art of Practice – an audio program on CD by
  Lance Giroux available from his website
  www.alliedronin.com

- The Lone Samurai – The Life of Miyamoto
  Musashi - by William Scott Wilson

- Bushido – The Soul of Japan - by Inazo Nitobe

- Conscious Business – by Fred Kofman

- The Four Agreements – by Don Miguel Ruiz

- Manual of the Warrior of the Light – by Paulo
  Coelho

# Book List 2

## Great Fantasy Writing:

- Of course, the 'Song of Ice and Fire' series by George R. R. Martin, also his collections of short fiction 'Dream Songs'

- Lord of the Rings by J. R. R. Tolkein

- The 3 trilogies by Robin Hobb
  - Assassin's
  - Liveship Traders
  - Fool's

- The Wheel of Time series by Robert Jordan

- The 'Magic of Recluse' series by L.E. Modesitt Jr.

- The Dresden Files series by Jim Butcher

- The Harry Potter series by J. K. Rowling

- The 'His Dark Materials' series by Phillip Pullman

- The Fencer Trilogy by K. J. Parker

- The Night Angel Trilogy by Brent Weeks

- The Way of Wyrd by Brian Bates

- Jonathan Strange and Mr. Norrell by Susanna Clark

- Any of the collections edited by Terry Windling

- The Wood-Wife by Terry Windling

- Anything by Neil Gaiman, but especially Stardust, and American Gods

I recognise that not all of this is 'High Fantasy', the sort with swords and dragons and stuff, but I'm not a purist and it is all great!

# Articles

I have included here some articles, mostly written originally for my blog, which I feel support, enhance, or enlarge upon what I have been writing about in this book. There are more on the blog and I'm writing more all the time so check it out:

The Warrior's Heart Blog: www.fudoshin.org.uk/blog

## Warrior's for Peace

It may seem odd to some to consider the Warrior archetype in conjunction with an orientation towards peace, however, I see the 2 things as not only linked but necessary to each other. One symbolic way of looking at the connection would be through the lens of Taoist beliefs that opposites create each other, as shown visually in the Yin Yang symbol – the black half contains the seed of the white half, and the white the seed of the black. In a slightly more concrete illustration, when I say yes to one thing I am simultaneously saying no to many other potential options. Yes and No are opposites but are interdependent upon one another.

To deal more specifically with the matter of the Warrior and Peace, a perfect example can be seen in The Samurai Game®. George Leonard who created The Samurai

Game® was a senior grade Aikido practitioner and former World War II fighter pilot. This was a man who had seen war and had deep experience of martial arts. He originally created the Game after he had met with a bunch of his old war buddies. They had all been reminiscing about their time together during the War and most of them had been saying that life had seemed dull by comparison since. This was not George's experience but it did set him to thinking about a question he had pondered often before: Why, when we know the consequences, do we continue to make war? There are many possible answers to this question ranging from the surface of any political considerations which are specific to each conflict but can be categorised as essentially being questions of power and control; right through to much deeper considerations of fundamental aspects of human nature. After many years of sitting with and experimenting with this question, one of the possible answers George came up with was:

Maybe it's just the juiciest game in town!

This could seem light or even crass, but pause for a minute. There is a part of the human psyche which craves vivid experience and as we have become increasingly 'developed' and 'civilised' this has become less and less nourished as time has gone on. When aspects of us which need expression are suppressed or ignored they will find ways to leak and burst out on their own. This is the nature of the human shadow. Maybe part of what keeps human beings making war is a basic craving for vivid experience. I think this is part of what George Leonard learned from running The Samurai Game® for many years, with all different kinds of groups. Certainly, part of what I see people coming into contact with through the Game is not only a deep connection with their own Warrior selves, but an experiential understanding of the consequences of war. This runs the range of very positive in that they have lived brightly, vividly, profoundly and completely connected to a higher purpose; right through to the truly terrible consequences of massive loss of life and ultimate futility. Here we have a fascinating dichotomy: a game about War where we learn profound and lasting lessons about Peace. In the modern world this is a rare, example of the beautiful balance of being a Warrior for Peace. Some martial arts dojo's manage to embrace and explore this but even there it is not as common as you might think.

In ancient times and indigenous cultures I think this marriage of Warriors working for Peace was more common. In many indigenous, tribal societies in recent history there were ritual ways of doing combat that limited the danger of loss of life. These were used to settle inter-tribal disputes but were often invoked and enacted at certain times of the year whether there was a conflict to settle or not. I see The Samurai Game® as being similar to this, and part of George Leonard's work to create a more vivid peace in the hope that we can one day relinquish war-making. When your community is smaller you notice the loss of one of you much more keenly – this is clear in The Samurai Game®, as I think it would be in smaller tribal village communities. I suspect death was in some ways a weightier matter in these communities than it is today in a world where we have such phrases as 'collateral damage' and 'acceptable losses.' In the arena of mass war, leaders have to numb themselves to the casualties or they will be overwhelmed.

Examples of the old ritualised combat forms are still visible today whether we draw a parallel between the mass bonding and vivid experience of war-time and sports events like football games, or we look to extant tribal communities and practices closely derived from them. Lacrosse began as a warrior game amongst first nation American's and was very much an arena for the young bucks of the tribe to let off steam and work out their aggressive urges in a contained environment. Many rites of passage and initiatory experiences were designed with a similar intention. As the saying goes "If the young men are not initiated they will burn down the village for warmth." I think this can be particularly true of young men but I think it is true for all of us that we need places where we can let our wild sides out of the box for a while. If we can find safe, contained ways of exercising our wilder nature, and aggressive tendencies then that is far preferable than risking hurting ourselves and others on a regular basis. This then becomes a conversation not just addressing external peace-making, but being at peace in ourselves – an issue which to look at the statistics about drug abuse, alcohol abuse, overeating, compulsive shopping and street violence is clearly a pressing issue for us to address both individually and culturally if we are to create a genuinely healthy society. To see some other examples of ritualised combat we can look at the Dundunbar rituals of West Africa (please forgive me if I have spelled this incorrectly, I have only heard it verbally described). Young men come together to do ritual combat with sticks. A great deal of pride and social recognition is at stake and while injuries can be serious it is nothing like the damage they would do if they were left to create real combat with heavier weapons. Capoeira is a martial art from Brazil that may have it's roots at least partially in the 'Zebra Dance' of Africa and is generally practised to avoid physical contact with a strong emphasis on ritual and an exercising of aggressive and competitive tendencies without doing harm. Part of the tradition of Capoeira is a dance called the 'Maculele' which is a ritualised dance-combat with sticks. One story I have heard about it is that originally it was a ritual created by 2 tribes who lived on either side of a valley. Once a year the 2 tribes would meet at the bottom of the valley and 'do battle' through the Maculele. Whether this story is historically correct or not, it is another example of ritual combat being used to alleviate the Warrior's call for real combat.

Whether we are looking at promoting inner peace or creating outer peace, it is clear to me that a healthy embrace and inclusion of the Warrior archetype in all of us is not only preferable but necessary.

For people who are seeking to be peace-workers themselves, I would see it as particularly important that they have not only studied peace but have learnt about and embraced their warrior selves. Otherwise, the potential that they will repress their aggressive tendencies is much greater. Aspects of ourselves which are repressed or 'left in shadow' in my experience not only leak out unconsciously in many small ways but also have a tendency to explode out at the most unfortunate moments. Imagine if you are working on a mediation case and one of the emotional dynamics pushes your buttons… It would be the worst possible moment for you as mediator to have an emotional explosion yourself! However, when our warrior tendencies, our need for healthy expression of anger, our need for vivid experience, and our need to be able to say "No" and draw hard boundaries when necessary have not been listened to, exercised and understood for long periods of time an emotional explosion is exactly what we are likely to get.

Even without the potential for unfortunate emotional outbursts or subtle emotional leakage, I think the Warrior has a fundamental role to play in creating Peace. To truly choose Peace we must be coming from a position of strength, other wise it is not something we are choosing, it is our last remaining option for survival. This idea is beautifully articulated by Paul Linden in his book 'Embodied Peacemaking' and by Daniele Bolelli in his book 'On the Warrior's Path.'

*"If Attila the Hun comes riding over the hill all set to pillage your village, the first, civilized step is to say, "Excuse me, Mr. Hun, but I'd really rather you not pillage my village." Of course, we know what he'd likely say. So the next step would be to make a clear statement of the negative consequences for him of his trying. And of course, we know what he would be likely to do. So the necessary last step would be physical self-defense. Without the capability of bottom-line, practical self-protection skills, other conflict resolution skills rest on a foundation of sand."*

*-Paul Linden*

*"You can only renounce what you are able to do. Peace is a choice only for those who are able to do battle. Otherwise, it's the desperate pleading of someone who has no alternatives. Unless you are a mean,*

*violent bastard with murderous tendencies to begin with, renouncing violence probably is not to the main thing on your mind when you pick up martial arts. Renouncing violence, anger, and aggression is a by-product of growing as a human being, of becoming more confident and secure in yourself. Once you are confident enough, you can afford to be sweet and open up emotionally to others because you are no longer afraid. Ultimately, mastering combat is a path to face one's fears and, at least partially, overcome them. Abandoning violent tendencies is only one of many transformations that take place when fear lessens its hold on us."*

*-Daniele Bolelli*

The Warrior and the Peacemaker may be apparent opposites, but like the Yin Yang symbol they are completely necessary to each other if we are to be whole people and if we are to create a more peaceful and loving world. They are not enemies, they are brothers. I think this is why so many great teachers through the ages have embraced the Warrior archetype while essentially teaching us to be more peaceful and loving: Chogyam Trungpa, Gichin Funakoshi, Morihei Ueshiba, George Leonard, Paul Linden, Richard Strozzi-Heckler, Paulo Coelho and many others. This too is why I do the work that I do.

# TV as Spiritual Practice

TV has a bad rap. That's not a new thing, when I was young and liked watching TV probably more than average my parents were concerned about it. I have since found out that it was particularly my Dad that was worried about it and when I went on to train to be an actor he realised that maybe there was some wisdom at play – I had started studying acting young! When I wrote this poem in my 20's my mum thought it was pretty funny:

<u>My Televisual Youth – a taste of things to come</u>

Oh lovely TV set

You're so warm and crumbly

Like a moist current bun

Just baked by my mum

Filling my tum

With a wholesome satisfaction

Playdays or World in Action

It's all the same to me

From my extra surrogate parent

That is the TV

Even the generation before my parents talked about the TV as the 'goggle-box' and said you'd get square eyes if you watched too much. In 'alternative' circles TV is often considered a very poor activity and if you say you don't have a TV you're celebrated! I should know: I don't have a TV – but… I do watch a fair amount of TV programs online.

Now I can understand disparaging TV for the amount of advertising shown and the way that breaks up the programs (although we've all gotta pay the bills right?), I also have to say I don't really get the huge flood of 'reality' shows there are going. Some have a kind of story arc I can understand, and Big Brother originally had a kind of psychological experiment cachet about it, but now? Still going? Really? All that said, some people love it and just because it's not for me doesn't mean it's wrong.

What I want to offer here is a different perspective on fictional TV – dramas, comedy, series, films, the whole bit, because I think they are often under-appreciated. The reason I think this is because I consider TV as a form of theatre. If you went and watched a play each evening, you would be considered fortunate indeed and pretty high-brow. If you watch TV each evening it's generally considered low-brow, if perhaps not unusual. One of the things that I think is under-appreciated is that many of the best theatrical writers today are writing for TV, some of them exclusively. Equally, many of the finest actors around are now working in television. It has been an increasing trend in the last 5 years or so that even actors who previously only worked in film have started working on TV series'. Some of the writing in TV series' is really powerful, deeply human, and very moving if you invest yourself in the story, engage with the characters and really allow yourself to be involved. David Mamet whose background as a writer is in theatre is one of the creators of 'The Unit', an American military action drama (which I have loved watching!). Tim Roth, one of the finest British actors of his generation (in my opinion) and successful film actor including working on cutting-edge pieces like the film version of Tom Stppard's 'Rosencrantz and Guildenstein are dead' is now the star in 'Lie to Me' a drama series drawing on Paul Ekman's psychological research. It is an excellent series, brilliantly written, characterised, acted and directed. This is some of the best contemporary story-telling going on.

I think the problem with TV is not the medium itself but how we use it. All too often I think that TV just serves as a background noise in the house to ensure there isn't silence. It can be a way not to spend time 'in my own company' and not to sit with thoughts and feelings on the inside. To quote from 'The Invitation' by Oriah Mountain Dreamer:

"I want to know if you can be alone with yourself, and if you truly like the company you keep in the empty moments"

The negative use of TV in my opinion is a way of ensuring I never have to answer this question.

This doesn't mean I'm against using TV for escapism. It can be wonderful to immerse myself in another world and someone else's cares, concerns, joys and adventures for an hour or two – so long as I don't do this all the time and lose touch with myself.   What I would propose is that by committing more fully, and escaping more deeply into the stories within your favourite TV you can find a path to a fuller and deeper relationship with yourself.

There is a technical term from theatre 'Suspension of disbelief.' This is something that as performers you have to work for. You have to create a world on the stage that is so inviting and immersing that the audience commit to suspending their disbelief for the duration of the play. They commit internally to believing in the world you have created on the stage so that the story lives as a theatrical truth for a while and has the power to move people emotionally rather than just being a body of lies.   In the theatre however, numerous ritual ties have been made to support suspension of disbelief before the play even begins: you have paid for a ticket, you have come together with lots of other people at a special time, many people dress up to go to the theatre, it's often a treat so you're invested in enjoying it, you come together in a special room and everyone makes an implicit agreement to be quiet while you all watch, at the end people know to clap their hands to show appreciation… when you think about it, going to the theatre is a highly ritualised act. From the point of view of the illusion of the story, TV today is better equipped than theatre ever has been.   It is on set's that are indistinguishable from day-to-day life and with the production budgets, lighting, and special effects it's completely believable.  But the ritual isn't there.  The TV gets thoughtlessly switched on and off, ignored, talked over, and spotting continuity errors seems for some people to virtually be a sport… really it doesn't stand much of a chance!   There is no commitment to suspension of disbelief. When you're creating a play you've got to do a good enough job to support people in suspension of disbelief, but in TV they've done the work. If you don't like it, don't watch it, but if you like watching something then do the artists who have put the work in to create this whole other world a favour and commit to the experience: Suspend your disbelief. Once you do this I genuinely believe that magic can happen. You can be transported to other worlds, but you can also vicariously experience emotions that you otherwise might leave buried.

In therapeutic work we talk about 'catharsis.' This is when someone has an experience of fully being in an emotion in a way that releases something for them – often something connected to a traumatic or difficult past experience. This kind of cathartic release can be very healing and can free up energy and attention in a way that no amount of talking about a life occurrence ever will. Not a lot of people know that the word 'Cathartic' has it's origins in classical Greek theatre. The ancient Greeks considered theatre to be a potentially healing experience and catharsis was when someone was able to allow themselves to feel something when they saw a character feeling it, that they couldn't feel on their own. I can certainly identify with some emotions felling almost too big for everyday life – if I am engaged and invested in a story about God's, Goddesses, Hero's and Heroines, then the context for the emotions is larger and it can feel safe to experience big emotions. Sometimes it is less painful to connect with a character's grief than it is to connect with my own, but that doesn't mean the tears I shed for the character are not also an emotional release for me. When my mother died, not long afterwards I saw a film called 'The Family Stone.' It is a beautiful film, very funny in places and the mother in the film (played wonderfully by Diane Keaton) really reminded me of my mum. It helped me to connect with my grief when I was at home, in my own space and snuggled up in a comfy jumper – the perfect environment! My experience with grief is that it can surface at any moment, and in response to the strangest things so it was a real relief to let some of my grief come, and to shed some tears after that film. It was much gentler for me to have those feelings in that moment than for them to suddenly surface while I was at the office or in the supermarket (both of which have happened).

The picture I'm trying to paint here is of Television as a true artistic medium, much like stage productions. For us to find the real benefit of it we need to engage with it more consciously. What TV requires of us is a commitment to suspension of disbelief. What TV offers us is the potential to really connect with that which is human within us and potentially to have a healing cathartic release of emotion.

So, "The Rev's" recommendation for spiritual and emotional exercise for today: curl up in front of your favourite TV program and immerse yourself in the world of the characters. Make a ritual of it, put on your favourite jumper, get a glass of your favourite drink (whatever floats your boat), and maybe some chocolate or ice-cream, switch off the phone, and get comfy. Spiritual practices don't have to be hard work! You never know what you might learn about yourself or what healing may happen as you sink into the world of the characters...

# Karate Begins and Ends with Rei

Gichin Funakoshi, the father of modern Karate defined 20 principles of Karate. There is much debate in the hard-core Karate fraternity about how true to the original form of Karate Funakoshi was, and others have questioned how great a fighter he was when compared with the likes of Kano (founder of Judo) or Ueshiba (founder of Aikido). However, whatever we think of Funakoshi's physical prowess, I consider him a true Warrior because of his commitment to his Way - his *Do*; and because he was a great philosopher and teacher. He was a Confucian scholar and, as was the case with many of the great martial teachers (including Kano and Ueshiba) he sought to teach his students a harmonious and compassionate way of life, not just a physical skill.

I wanted to 'unpack' the 20 principles of Karate so that they can be applied to the whole of life and not just to Karate. I will do this 1 at a time and will drop them into this blog over the coming weeks and months. Here is the first:

## Karate Begins and ends with Rei

*Rei* is the word used to denote the formal Japanese bow that you will see a lot in traditional Dojo's (Dojo is the name for a training hall and means 'place of the Way'). *Rei* also means respect. Karate classes literally begin and end with a bow, as do all engagements with an opponent, but what I think we are being reminded of here is more relating to the symbolic aspect of this practice than the literal. The constant bowing in martial arts classes can be seen as just cultural garnish, keeping the art 'Japanese flavoured.' However, I see it as a vital part of our practice. Bowing is a practice of humility. We are bodily offering deep respect and gratitude to whoever and whatever we are bowing to. I say whatever, because traditionally the Dojo would have had a Shinto shrine which would have been the first and the last thing we would bow to. This shrine was, amongst other things, the home of the spirit of the land and building it was in. As such, when we bow to this shrine, we are offering our respects to the place we are training in, and in my mind, this also means the land itself. Indeed, with Shinto being a religion which recognises many spirits of nature, I think that this respect would traditionally have extended out to the land and the natural surroundings. This reminder of respect for our environment is perhaps more important now than ever. With the damage that has been done and continues to be done to the natural world, we must bring this awareness to every day of our lives if we are going to leave an inhabitable world for our children and their children.

The other bow that comes at the beginning and end of the class is to the Sensei. They are the teacher but with some subtle differences. Sensei means 'one who has gone before' so it is someone who has walked the path we are setting our feet on so they can help us find our way safely and can set the pace so that we are constantly challenged. Of course it is important to respect our teachers, but also, my feeling is that when we bow to the outward Sensei, we also have the opportunity to bow to our inner Sensei. There is a part of us which is naturally connected to a deep wisdom and it is this part of ourselves that makes our learning possible as much as any external teacher or guide. There is also the opportunity to remind ourselves to be grateful for all our teachers, even the people and events in our lives which are difficult. It is a reminder that all experience has something to teach us.

So when we bow, when we *rei,* we are physically reminding ourselves of our gratitude for the beauty of the world around us; the challenge and learning offered by all of our opponents in life (internal and external); the humbling wisdom which lies in the teaching we receive from others and ourselves; and we are reminding ourselves to bring the quality of respect to every moment. Gratitude, humility, respect: Karate-do begins and ends in *rei.*

You don't need to go to a Karate class to practice *Rei.* If you have a meditation practice you can begin that and end it with a bow of some kind and bring this awareness to your practice. If you don't have a practice already then you could take up bowing as a practice. It only takes a few moments and it is a wonderful way of bodily invoking these qualities of gratitude, humility and respect. So, maybe when you first get up in the morning, or when you enter and leave your house or living room you could take a moment to centre yourself and make a really conscious bow. Remember, you are bowing to the world, your immediate environment, yourself as you are, the 'master' that lives within you, and all those opponents you have faced and will face who are teachers for you if only you can discern the lesson.

# There is no first strike in Karate

This is the second of Gichin Funakshi's 20 principles of Karate. This has often been interpreted as meaning that while Karate is primarily a form of self-defence (not offence), the true Karate practitioner will be so aware and so fast that as soon as they detect an attack, they strike with such swiftness and certainty that while both combatants move together, the Karate-ka strikes the winning blow. I think this is at least a little shallow, and considering Funakoshi was a Confucian scholar and a deeply contemplative individual, I'd like to think he intended a deeper reading of it too. So here's my interpretation...

### There is no first strike in Karate

What this means to me is that Karate is about relationship. When I sit in a place of judgement I can say "you started it, it's your fault!" or "I struck first, I won." But if I see everything as a form of interconnected relationship then there is no blame and no winner: somehow 'we' create the moment where conflict or achievement occurs. Karate should be first and foremost an awareness discipline. The teaching of 'self defence techniques' is, I believe, misleading. There is the whole issue of what a fight really looks like (which is frankly very ugly) as compared with what is often taught (which is choreographed). I have often seen people (including myself at times) walk out of a dojo with a greatly inflated sense of skill when dealing with 'real fighting.' This is dangerous because this attitude will tend to make you more, not less likely to get into a fight. It is important to gain a sense of physical self confidence, and some studies have been done that seem to suggest that career criminals instinctively steer clear of people who are grounded and centred regardless of their size or sex (these are cited in George Leonard's book 'The Way of Aikido'). So learning to be grounded and centred, to have sufficient physical awareness and confidence that your physicality does not say "victim" is an important learning and may prevent trouble in the first place. The attitude that goes with "I can take care of myself" tends more towards some arrogance or even mild aggression – which is more likely to attract the attention of a certain kind of trouble-maker. In these examples the 'first strike' has gone from being a physical act to an attitudinal stance. Without necessarily being aware of it, in thinking 'I can take care of myself' I walk around projecting subtle 'what are you looking at?!' vibes. I have been very fortunate to train with wise and subtle teachers (both physically and through reading some excellent books) who have encouraged me towards a deep kind of physical awareness rather than focusing on the fight. I believe it is this kind of physical awareness which should be at the heart of what we learn in Karate (or any martial art for that matter), and is also at the heart of what I consider to be 'self defence.' Even once someone seems to have engaged with us aggressively (which most commonly begins verbally), how we respond to that mentally, emotionally, and physically, can have a huge impact on whether the situation escalates. In this way, there is no point we can call the 'first strike' because every situation is an environment where many subtle forces are interacting moment to moment. This interaction begins at the subconscious level so the more aware we can be of what is going on in ourselves, in the world around us and the interface between the two, the better we can become at ensuring a first strike never becomes necessary (whether that 'strike' as an act of aggression is physical, mental or emotional).

The Kanji (Japanese writing, based on Chinese characters) for *Budo* which means 'warrior way' is made up of 2 other Kanji: one which means 'halberds', the other means 'to stop.' So the root of the warrior path is to stop combat happening. This gives us a different idea of what it means to be a warrior than most of the popular films portray for us, and it is from this perspective that I interpret Gichin Funakoshi's second principle. With this at the heart of our understanding of the warrior way, we become warriors of compassion, warriors of peace.

I have mentioned a 'Way' or path a number of times and the introduction from my first book explains a bit about what that means and where the concept comes from. So I have included that here. Some people may think that a book like this is geeky. Some may think that loving fantasy fiction and spending many hours or even years training in obscure and archaic fighting methods is basically for nerds. Well, the first chapter of my first book has something to say about that so I offer that here too...

# Introduction: The Way

We all want to be good at something. Let's face it, most of us who haven't had all the passion squeezed out of us want to be <u>really</u> good at something. It almost doesn't matter what the thing is – just to be that good, to be able to say "I'm World-class." But how do we envision this goal? I'd say that in the western world we have a pretty limited idea of what achievement really means. It mostly seems to mean Bigger, Faster, Stronger, Taller, just plain MORE! I think there's another way...

It's a way that has been around in the West forever but has only been applied to certain disciplines (primarily the arts). It has been suggested by certain modern and progressive psychologies. But I think it has been best explored and expressed in the Far East where it has been inherent in some of their oldest philosophical approaches. What is that way? Good question.

It is **The *Way.*** It has it's roots in Taoism (an ancient Chinese religion and spiritual path) and found further expression in Japanese Zen Buddhism. '*Tao*' (sometimes *Dao*) in Chinese or '*Do*' in Japanese translates as '*Way*.' So when I say it's The *Way*, that's what I mean – The *Way* as in The *Tao*, or The *Do*. 'The *Way*' in Taoism and the *Do*-forms in Japan are practices like martial arts, or calligraphy, or brush-painting but they are much more than just an activity, they are the medium through which the practitioner meditates, explores the nature of the universe, and creates the most fundamental expression of how they live their life! These are not just hobbies, they are life practices. I think, if the ancient Chinese could turn flower-arranging into a *Way*, then why not turn anything into a *Way*? So this book is not just about doing stuff it's about *Do*-ing stuff: taking something you **do** and making it a **Do** (see how beautifully I've set up that pun? That's part of my *Way*, I learnt it from my Dad).

The *Way* is not about Bigger, Faster, Stronger, Taller or More. It is about someone expressing their essential nature. It is about blossoming into the fullness of your being – and not in an 'I'm the most beautiful blossom ever' kinda way – in a 'finding out who you are and living that' kinda way. When you really do that, as the song says, nobody does it better.

This is not about converting you to some religion, making you shave your head, selling you a line of 'The *Way*'™ T-shirts, or selling your Soul to Santa. It could be described as a spiritual path but only in so much as it is a path and if you want to you can involve your spiritual self in the journey. That's all up to you. My personal experience is that by taking certain activities and bringing a special mindset to them I have learned about myself and found a deeper sense of who I really am. It's not any kind of objective truth (if such a thing exists) but it has brought me joy in the good times and peace in the tough times and that's good enough for me.

The *Way* is not really about the activities that help to cultivate it. The *Way* is your unique path in the world. When that's really written in your heart then you can experience all kinds of *Ways* and all kinds of people and they all help to feed you in your own *Way*. In the words of the Hagakure[24]:

> *"It is bad when one thing becomes two. One should not look for anything else in the Way of the Samurai. It is the same for anything that is called a Way. Therefore it is inconsistent to hear something of the Way of Confucius or the Way of the Buddha, and say that this is the Way of the Samurai. If one understands things in this manner, he should be able to hear about all Ways and be more and more in accord with his own."*

For this reason I think anything can be a *Way*. That's what this book is about – helping you to find an activity you love enough to really work at it and then developing it into a *Way*.

---

24 Hagakure, The Book of the Samurai by Yamamoto Tsunetomo, Translated by William Scott Wilson

# Chapter 1:
# All Zen Masters are Geeks and Anoraks![25]

I think one of the reasons why we view mastery and excellence as we do in the West is because of school: In school it's not cool to be good at stuff unless it's mainstream. This will probably depend on the school but at my school, being good at football was cool. Sports were generally a cool thing to be good at but Football was top of the pile. Music might be cool to be good at... guitar was cool, oboe was not. As we got older and moved towards driving age, knowing a lot about cars was cool. Being academically strong was not cool, but particularly maths, the sciences and history were not cool. Religious Studies didn't even get on the radar. These are mostly examples from the boys side of the fence and from my school in particular but most of us develop a sixth sense about what's cool and what's not when we are at school and I'm sure you can fill in your own examples.

---

25 Since first starting to work on this book it has come to my attention that people outside of the UK have no idea what 'Anorak' means! So, to explain: an anorak is technically speaking a type of water-proof jacket – maybe like a wind-cheater in the US? However, when applied as a label for a person it indicates that they are passionately, almost obsessively interested in something which involves a high degree of technical knowledge. Usually it is something which is not cool to like, let alone love. In the UK a train-spotter or stamp-collector might be seen as an 'Anorak.' A pop-culture reference could be the character Ross from 'Friends' and how he's always correcting people about obscure details to do with dinosaurs. Hope that helps!

In this environment where only certain activities are safe to be enthusiastic about, is it any wonder that many of us loose our way? In the rarefied social environment of the playground or the sports field or the canteen you just didn't say "You know what? I love Renaissance poetry!" If you did you were a geek. Likewise, it would have been a special kind of social suicide to say "This algebra stuff is brilliant, I could just play with numbers and letters like this all day!" If you did you were an anorak.

Most of us will have had relatively little safe space growing up to explore what really excited us. We have been socially educated to hide away any passions which don't 'fit the mould' of our peer group.

I think that to find our *Way* we have to love something. It's not always the case but I've often found that the things I fall in love with are things I have some natural talent for. That doesn't mean I find them easy – the challenge is part of what gets me really hooked long-term – but when I first try it there's a zing of recognition like I've done it before and the process of learning is more like a 'remembering'.

I never really learnt to love football, but it wouldn't surprise me if many of my school friends did. They learnt to love it but I suspect only a handful loved it straight away. In my heart there were other things I loved straight away, and some of them have taken years to discover. Most of the things I love would have definitely placed me in the Geek-camp at school. Karate was one of them, but not the high kicking, cool 'Karate Kid' Karate, no.... A rare form of old Okinawan Karate that is compact and probably not that impressive to watch. Another example would be a love of world religions and philosophies. Definitely not cool where

I came from. My most recent discovery is 'Card Scaling'. "What is that?!" I hear you cry. It is the skill of throwing playing cards with enough power to stick in a water-melon or fly for hundreds of feet. Throwing playing cards like a ninja! Sound kinda geeky? Fair enough, but I love it.

It is interesting to note how people in the East who obsessively train in obscure disciplines are given titles of respect, while in the West they are called Geeks and Anoraks. Take a Zen master as an example. He (or she) spends years sitting still. Their other key activity is contemplating ancient pieces of short and confusing poetry. It sounds like a geek and smells like a geek, it's a geek! Ancient poetry that doesn't have any immediate or obvious meaning?! What an anorak!

If you want to master something, if you want to find a *Way* that will nourish you and help you grow it's got to be something that lives in your heart; and that means that, by the world's standards, it might not be cool.

There are *Ways* already defined and laid out for you to pick up: the martial arts, Zen flower arranging, calligraphy, brush painting, pottery, carving, the Japanese tea ceremony. That's not what this book is about. What I'm looking to do here is set out some principles so that you can take any activity and turn it into a *Way*. Hell, if the Samurai and monks of ancient Japan could turn making the tea into a Zen art then why shouldn't we be able to do the same with anything? Wine tasting is virtually there already but it could be anything: Cake baking, accountancy, the application of make-up, dog walking, throwing stones into the sea – anything!

If you're going to undertake this task and find a *Way* for yourself you'd better get in touch with your inner geek.

Revere the anorak in your heart. These are the parts of you that are capable of completely investing themselves in the deep, deep detail of their activities no matter what anyone else thinks. And remember that all Zen masters are Geeks and Anoraks.

# Author Profile

Francis trained originally as an actor, then ran away from the circus to find his home. He has trained in a wide range of martial arts over the years including European medieval weaponry, Karate, Tai Chi, Capoeira, Iaido, Hsing Yi, I Chuan, Aikido, and he has a 3$^{rd}$ Dan black belt in Kodo Ryu Karate. He has studied philosophical and spiritual paths from around the world with a special interest in the indigenous traditions of the land, and philosophy which grows out of a warrior's life.

These days he is primarily a workshop leader, facilitator, writer and Interfaith Minister. He particularly enjoys facilitating The Samurai Game® (originally created by George Leonard) for which he is currently the only certified facilitator in the UK. It is in facilitating this wonderful Game that he gets to take on the role of 'War God' in case you saw that on the cover and wondered how *that* might work! He offers workshops and trainings exploring the warrior archetype, leadership, embodiment, presence, and spirituality. He specialises in somatic (working with the body), and experiential training methods.

He lives in Brighton, UK with his wife and son. Francis loves the sea especially in the Autumn when it's stormy and dramatic.

If you'd like to know more about his work, find some free resources, do an online course or read Francis' blog go to:

**www.fudoshin.org.uk**

i   From 'The Hedge Knight', published in the anthology 'Dream Songs' by George R. R. Martin, Pub. Gollancz

ii  Also from 'The Hedge Knight'

iii From 'A Storm of Swords 1: Steel and Snow' by George R. R. Martin, Pub. Harper Voyager

iv  This version is taken from 'Kishido – The Way of the Western Warrior' by Peter Hobart, Pub. Hohm Press

v   Taken from 'Bushido: The Soul of Japan' by Inazo Nitobe, Pub. Kodansha

vi  'The Hagakure' is by Yamamoto Tsunetomo and the best known translation is by William Scott Wilson, Pub. Kodansha

vii This translation taken from 'The Twenty Guiding Principles of Karate: The Spiritual Legacy of the Master' by Gichin Funakoshi, Jotaro Takagi, and Translated by John Teramoto. Pub. Kodansha USA

viii Version taken from 'Kishido'

ix  I certainly heard Simon quote this to me and I believe it is also in his beautiful book, "The Shamanic Way of the Bee" by Simon Buxton, pub. Bear Publishing

x   From 'In Search of the Warrior Spirit' by Richard Strozzi Heckler, Pub. North Atlantic Books

xi  From 'Conscious Business' by Fred Kofman, Pub. Sounds New

xii Quote taken from Episode 2 of the HBO Game of Thrones series, season 1. I will reference all subsequent quotes by episode number only

xiii Taken from Episode 1

xiv Quotes taken from scene in Episode 5

xv  This is the title of a book of quotes collated by students of the late Shunryu Suzuki and relates to a moment in a talk he once gave about how everything is perfect, and... that doesn't mean that things aren't still improved by a little polishing!

xvi The incident is in Episode 2, while the conversation between Ned and Arya happens in Episode 3

xvii Taken from Episode 1

xviii Taken from Episode 4

xix Quote from scene in Episode 4

xx  Taken from Episode 3

xxi Taken from Episode 7

xxii Quote taken from 'Shambhala: The Sacred Path of the Warrior' by Chogyam Trungpa, Pub. Shambhala Publications, Inc.

xxiii Quote taken from the 7th Chapter of Hagakure – The Book of the Samurai By Yamamoto Tsunetomo, Translated by William

Scott Wilson, Pub. Kodansha

xxiv Quote taken from the 1$^{st}$ Chapter Of Hagakure, as above.

xxv Quote taken from 'The Way of the Peaceful Warrior' By Dan Millman, Pub. HJKramer

xxvi Scene described and quotes from a scene in Episode 2

xxvii Taken from Episode 8

xxviii Quote taken from 'How to Save Your Own Life' by Erica Jong, Pub. Bloomsbury Publishing

xxix Taken from Episode 3

xxx Taken from Episode 1

xxxi This takes place in Episode 2

xxxii Taken from a scene in Episode 3

xxxiii Quote taken from the 1$^{st}$ Chapter Of Hagakure, as above.

xxxiv Taken from Episode 7

xxxv Taken from Episode 3

xxxvi Taken from Episode 5

xxxvii Taken from a scene in Episode 6

xxxviii Quote taken from 7$^{th}$ Chapter of Hagakure, as above.

xxxix Taken from Episode 8

xl   Both quotes taken from Scene in Episode 5

xli  This is often stated by the character 'Lan Mandragoran' in Robert Jordan's epic fantasy series 'The Wheel of Time'

xlii Taken from a scene in Episode 6

xliii Taken from a scene in Episode 6

xliv Quote taken from the 10$^{th}$ Chapter of the Hagakure, as above.

xlv Quote taken from the 10$^{th}$ Chapter of the Hagakure, as above.

xlvi Taken from Episode 5

xlvii Taken from Episode 3

xlviii Taken from Episode 7

xlix Taken from Episode 2

l    Taken from Episode 6

li   All taken from Episode 7

lii  Taken from Episode 1

liii Quote taken from 'Kishido' as above.

liv Taken from Episode 3

lv I no longer have the article to properly reference but I know it was in an edition of 'What is Enlightenment' Magazine (now re-named 'Enlightenext') which had a theme about masculinity.

lvi Taken from Episode 3

lvii Taken from Episode 3

lviii This is apparently from the Hagakure but is taken from a quote in 'On the Warrior's Path' by Daniele Bolelli, Pub. Blue Snake

Books

lix  Taken from Episode 4

lx   Quote taken from 'On the Warrior's Path' by Daniele Bolelli, Pub. Blue Snake Books

lxi  Quote taken from 'In Search of the Warrior Spirit' by Richard Strozzi Heckler – see above

lxii Taken from Episode 3

lxiii Quote taken from 'The Social Animal' by David Brooks, Pub. Short Books Ltd.

lxiv Taken from Episode 4

lxv  Taken from a scene in Episode 8

lxvi Taken from a scene in Episode 8

lxvii Both these quotes taken from a scene in Episode 5

lxviii Taken from Episode 4

lxix Quote taken from 'A Fighter's Heart' by Sam Sheridan, Pub. Atlantic Books

lxx  Quote from Charles Edward Montague's essay 'Disenchantment' which contains his reflection of the First World War

# Warriors of Love Publishing

Warriors of Love Publishing is a branch of Fudoshin Development. We are looking to produce new works on personal and spiritual development. We are passionate about human potential, spiritual growth and books! We want to publish work that will help encourage the kind of shift in consciousness that is sorely needed to repair the relationship between human beings, other human beings, and Mother Earth.

It may seem a joke to say we are passionate about books, but it's true. We love books. Not just as repositories of knowledge and catalysts of understanding but as objects. There's something wonderful about books that e-books, e-readers, and the Kindle will never replace.

If you'd like to make orders over 5 copies in the UK or want to get in touch, go to:

www.fudoshin.org.uk

CPSIA information can be obtained
at www.ICGtesting.com
Printed in the USA
LVOW13s1058221216
518415LV00007B/508/P